RAILWAYS AND THE DALES

DAVID JOY

PHOTOGRAPHY

GAVIN MORRISON

GREAT-N-ORTHERN

Great Northern Books
PO Box 1380, Bradford, BD5 5FB
www.greatnorthernbooks.co.uk

ISBN: 978-1-914227-20-2

Design and layout: David Burrill

CIP Data
A catalogue for this book is available from the British Library

CONTENTS

PREFACE

Over forty years have elapsed since I first compiled a book featuring the outstanding railway photography of Gavin Morrison. In 1981 I was an editor at Dalesman Publishing, developing a list that in theory covered all aspects of the Yorkshire Dales but inevitably became slanted towards my obsession with railways. British Rail had just revealed its intention to close the wildly improbable Settle & Carlisle line – and it suddenly seemed to be in its final years.

There was now an insatiable demand for books on the line and the result was a series of photo albums beginning with *Steam on the Settle & Carlisle*. There was certainly no shortage of submitted illustrations, but Gavin quickly came to occupy pride of place. I had no hesitation in deciding that the frontispiece should be his portrayal of 'Jubilee' *Leander* storming through Dent station. It epitomised steam in all its glory on the heights of the Dales and a skilled ability to depict trains in the landscape rather than just shots of locomotives.

Gavin went on to supply photos for subsequent Settle & Carlisle albums and books on railways in other parts of northern England. Unlike many photographers, he did not give up and put his cameras away when 'real' steam finished in 1968. Instead, he has continued to capture the changing railway scene up to the present day. A collection of some 200,000 pictures is not only amazing in extent but is also held on a digital database. Gavin can usually find any photograph within a couple of minutes!

Frequently a harassed editor's salvation, he has continued to meet numerous challenging requests down the years. We felt it was time to mark four decades of working together and take a radically different approach in a new book on railways and the Dales. Rather than my completing the text before selecting the photos, Gavin would first choose his favourite images and I would then write detailed captions for each picture along with introductory reading. We have found that taking a fresh perspective has been immensely rewarding for two Yorkshiremen who have the highest regards for the Dales.

Sadly, many lines had gone before the age of colour photography. They are included in my earlier paperback (see list of further reading on page 128). In this present book, over 150 photos extend back to 1958 – a year representing a lull before steam power was widely ousted in favour of dieselisation. Ironically, the line that has proved most difficult is the Settle & Carlisle. Its likely demise and eventual reprieve made it what may well be the most photographed railway in Britain. Such status is certainly deserved but has tended to overshadow other lines with many worthy features. There were times when we felt the best approach would be to omit it altogether, but instead made a firm decision to limit coverage to no more than a third of the book. We were determined to capture all railways of the Dales in their immense variety and feel this has been achieved.

David Joy
January 2022

INTRODUCTION

True northerners should need no explanation, as to them 'the Dales' unquestionably means the Yorkshire Dales. It is quite simply a glorious corner of what has become known as 'God's Own County'. To avoid any doubt, this book uses 'the Dales' to mean the area and 'dales' for its various river valleys. Seven of them feature in these pages – Airedale, Ribblesdale, Dentdale, Garsdale, Wharfedale, Nidderdale and Wensleydale.

In photos dating back to 1958 the distinction between the two groups of railways that served them was still self-evident. Created by the Midland and then becoming part of the LMS was a mainline out of Leeds through Airedale to Skipton and Settle before climbing up Ribblesdale. Viaducts and tunnels then took it high above Dentdale and Garsdale before a long descent down Mallerstang and past Kirkby Stephen to Carlisle. Many of the locomotives and stations clearly reflected its Midland Railway origins. So too did its branches running deeper into the Dales to Ilkley and Grassington.

Quite different was a second main line out of Leeds completed in 1849 almost thirty years before it became overshadowed by the more famous Settle & Carlisle. At the time it was a great engineering achievement, as it had to penetrate the ridge between Airedale and Wharfedale through what at over two miles was then Britain's third longest railway tunnel. Edging round Harrogate and Ripon, it bridged the rivers Nidd, Ure and Swale to join the East Coast mainline at Northallerton. Becoming part of the North Eastern Railway and then the LNER, it also left no doubt as to its origins. In Nidderdale it connected with a line to Knaresborough and York as well as a branch to Pateley Bridge.

There were still signs that the two companies had been uneasy neighbours.

A North Eastern branch along Wharfedale shared tracks with the Midland into Ilkley but it was never an entirely harmonious arrangement. There was also a straggling North Eastern line up Wensleydale that met a branch from the Settle & Carlisle in an unlikely 'frontier' station at Hawes. To keep ancient rites alive, the branch latterly handled one inconveniently timed train a day until it finally succumbed in 1959. It survived just long enough to feature in the final pages of this book.

Misplaced optimism that had been a hallmark of branches into the Dales had already taken its toll. Passenger services to Grassington lasted only 28 years and ceased in 1930. Other casualties were those to Pateley Bridge in 1951 and from Northallerton to Hawes three years later. Yet there were also hopeful signs such as the pioneer introduction of diesel multiple units [DMUs] between Leeds and Harrogate in 1954. They ran to a much-improved timetable, paving the way for similar changes to Airedale and Wharfedale services in 1959.

Positive developments then gave way to serious decline. The infamous Beeching Report soon led to closure of lines from Leeds via Otley to Ilkley and onwards through Bolton Abbey to Skipton. More serious was the loss of a mainline when passenger services north of Harrogate through Ripon to Northallerton ended in 1967.

The 1960s also saw the demise of railways that had continued to handle a diminishing number of goods trains. Quarry traffic kept the Grassington branch open to Swinden and the Wensleydale line as far as Redmire, but there was no similar source of revenue to justify a few wagons trundling up Nidderdale to Pateley Bridge.

Most goods depots on remaining lines closed, as in 1965 did all the smaller intermediate passenger stations between Leeds and Skipton. Five years later the same fate befell the Settle & Carlisle. Demolition of surplus station buildings, coupled with the end of aging steam locomotives and wholesale removal of surplus sidings, signalling and sundry facilities, took away much of the former character of railways serving the Dales. Within two decades a clear distinction between ex Midland and former North Eastern lines had gone.

The 1970s brought new opportunities coupled with mixed feelings. Although never fully accepted by diehards, the Yorkshire Ridings that had existed for a thousand years came to an end with local government reorganisation in 1974. A new West Yorkshire Metropolitan County had a Passenger Transport Executive (mercifully soon known as the PTE). It was responsible for many commuter services including those out of Leeds to Skipton, Ilkley and beyond its borders to Harrogate. The eventual result was greatly improved rolling stock, a far higher frequency of trains and several new or reopened stations.

The line to Ilkley via Guiseley had come close to succumbing prior to this new era, only escaping closure through sheer determination by a local action group. Their efforts foreshadowed a far greater campaign that now gradually gathered strength to save what is unquestionably the greatest railway the Dales has ever known. The extraordinary events of the 1980s that culminated in a reprieve for the Settle & Carlisle remain the stuff of drama and should never be forgotten. If nothing else, they meant that rail closures were firmly off the political agenda.

In the context of the Dales, the future was now set and its railway network firmly established. Road congestion has led to greatly increased use of the West Yorkshire Metro lines, boosted in 1995 by electrification from Leeds to Skipton and, amazingly, on the once doomed Ilkley branch.

Preservation schemes began in 1988 with what is now the Embsay & Bolton Abbey Steam Railway followed in 2003 by the Wensleydale Railway, initially between Leeming Bar and Leyburn. Both lines serve the Yorkshire Dales National Park, as do bus services often connecting with trains from such gateway towns as Skipton, Ilkley and Harrogate. The huge growth in passenger numbers on the Settle & Carlisle is coupled with linked walks among mountain scenery of the highest calibre and a desire to experience one of the world's great rail journeys. Collectively railways and the Dales have come to play a key part in an age of leisure with virtually all surviving lines offering their best-ever services. They continue to provide a photographer's dream ticket.

AIREDALE

LEEDS TO SKIPTON

Well before railways, it was canals that gave Airedale vital importance. It provided the lowest of all possible crossings of the Pennines, with the Aire Gap forming a route from Yorkshire into Lancashire that scarcely exceeded the 500ft contour. The idea of using Airedale for a waterway 'uniting the east and west seas' caught the imagination of investors. By the 1770s the Leeds & Liverpool Canal had reached Skipton and on to Gargrave before turning south to Colne and Burnley. It provided transport for numerous cotton mills, transforming local trade and blighting a valley hitherto on a par with Wharfedale for the clean waters of its river, its woods and rich farming land.

The Leeds & Liverpool Canal proved astonishingly prosperous for both mill owners and shareholders. Small wonder that following the same route was a tempting prospect for railway promoters. Masterminded by George Hudson, a line paralleling the waterway was opened in 1846 from Leeds to Shipley as part of an indirect route to Bradford. Never far from the canal, it continued through Keighley and Skipton to give an end-on junction with Lancashire lines in Colne. Completed in 1848, it was quickly absorbed by the powerful Midland Railway based in Derby.

The railway accelerated industrial development begun by the canal. Green grass gave way to mill chimneys – a change lamented by the Archbishop of Canterbury: 'The whole valley from end to end is spoiled, enslaved, dejected. It was the very home and spring of fresh air and water, and now it is a sewer of smoke, with a mantling ditch.' Airedale no longer stood any comparison with the scenic glories of Wharfedale and became more commonly known as the Aire Valley. Only in recent times has the 'dale' suffix been considered a marketable commodity and it has reverted to its original name.

From the outset the railway was seen as a means of providing a brief escape from smoke and misery. It had scarcely been opened when Keighley Mechanics' Institute organised an excursion on Whit Monday 1849 to Skipton, from where participants could walk across to the canal. Boats then took them to the grounds of Eshton Hall near Gargrave on the edge of the Dales. Special arrangements were made to provide a band and inclusive tickets for the 'male and female classes'.

Later that year four bands were engaged by Titus Salt, Bradford's biggest employer, when he took some two thousand of his workforce deeper into the Dales. What the local paper described as 'a monster train' of 41 carriages drawn by two locomotives was followed by another of more sensible length. They reached the station known as 'Bell Busk for Malham', even though this jewel among spectacular limestone country was four miles away. It was not a problem when walking long distances was part of everyday life.

Bell Busk was on the line extending north-west from Skipton. It too was absorbed by the Midland Railway as an integral part of its bid to reach an Irish Sea port – initially at Morecambe. This line passed through Clapham, the junction for an intended Anglo-Scottish mainline that was superseded by the improbable Settle-Carlisle railway.

These developments are described later in this book, but Titus Salt undoubtedly belongs to Airedale. In 1853 he combined all his textile operations in the vast Salt's Mill alongside the railway a mile west of Shipley. With its five storeys, lavish amounts of glass and Italianate bell towers, it was a world away from the traditional dark and satanic milltown image. It formed part of the 'model town' of Saltaire, catering for the social and spiritual welfare of its inhabitants, with Titus taking the view that they had no need to go elsewhere. Three years elapsed before they were provided with a station.

The heyday of Aire Valley services in Edwardian days saw through expresses from London St Pancras to both Glasgow and Edinburgh, as well as the evening 'residential' that took wool magnates home from Bradford to Morecambe and included an exclusive club car. There was a gradual decline in status following the Grouping of 1923 when the Midland became part of the LMS and played second string to the West Coast mainline from London Euston to Scotland.

Change for the better came in January 1959 when DMUs took over local services, but there was then a series of setbacks in the post-Beeching era. Only Bingley and Keighley remained open when other intermediate stations between Leeds and Skipton were closed in March 1965. At Skipton a truly short-sighted move saw closure of the line to Colne. It was only ten miles long and cost savings must have been minimal. Its retention could have put Airedale towns within reach of the highly successful Manchester Metro running out to Bury. Anglo-Scottish services also ebbed away and eventually met their demise as part of the scheming to close the Settle-Carlisle line.

The pendulum finally started to swing the other way following formation in 1974 of the West Yorkshire PTE. The value of rail travel versus congested roads was at last being recognised. By the mid-1980s it had provided platforms for Leeds to Skipton services on the Shipley triangle, opened a new park-and-ride station at Crossflatts a mile west of Bingley and re-opened Saltaire almost twenty years after its closure. The real plus came in September 1995 with a greatly improved new timetable following electrification. Half-hour interval workings from both Leeds and Bradford gave Airedale the best level of services it had ever seen.

THE OLD ORDER

Above

A scene symbolic of a vanished age sixty years ago and a railway used by many travellers to reach the Yorkshire Dales. Leaving Leeds City station on 6th March 1962 is the 1.54pm service to Carnforth. Manual signals are still in use, electrification with overhead wires is far into the future and the industrial haze means that the Queen's Hotel is only faintly visible in the background. There are no high-rise buildings.

The train will call at Keighley and then Skipton, where there were connecting buses to Grassington and the heart of the Dales. It would continue through increasingly spectacular countryside, with open views of the great mountain peak of Ingleborough, before reaching its destination.

With steam haulage on British Railways ending in 1968, Jubilee class No. 45730 *Ocean* is in its final phase of active passenger service.

Opposite, above

There was still plenty of freight traffic in August 1962, as typified by this long goods train easing out of Bingley. It is heading towards the point where the local animal market was then situated and is now Crossflatts park-and-ride station. The mill in the background has long been occupied by the internationally acclaimed firm of Damart.

Stanier 8F 2-8-0 No. 48084 was for many years allocated to sheds in the Leeds and Wakefield area.

Below

A portent of changes to come in a location that is now unrecognisable. This April 1961 view looks towards Calverley & Rodley station with its main buildings on the overbridge in the background. The station closed four years later on 25th March 1965 and there is now just a double-track electrified mainline carrying services with a frequency that would then have seemed inconceivable. Long gone are goods sidings and the Midland Railway signal box on the extreme left.

With steam power about to give way to diesel haulage, class 40 No. D258 is returning with a daily crew-training run from Leeds to Appleby and back. Hence the non-corridor carriages, although a few years earlier decrepit rolling stock of this kind was commonly used on excursion trains from Leeds to Morecambe for the famous Illuminations. After much alcoholic refreshment, the return journey must have been challenging!

On the right are carriages that spent virtually the entire year languishing in the sidings before being pressed into use on summer Saturdays and Bank Holidays. Harsh economics and intense use of the railway and its rolling stock had yet to prevail.

THE THAMES-CLYDE EXPRESS

Above

Nothing more strikingly conveys changes to the Airedale mainline than the fate of the Thames-Clyde Express. Named as a titled train back in 1927, it was the premier service over the Midland route from London St Pancras to Carlisle and on to Glasgow. Running non-stop between Leeds and Carlisle, it in no sense served the Dales but it gave its passengers a magnificent journey.

There was a definite sense of occasion when it passed at speed through stations such as Keighley and Skipton.

On 9th March 1961 the Thames-Clyde Express was still steam-hauled and A3 No. 60082 *Neil Gow* is seen in fine style passing the now demolished Kirkstall power station on the outskirts of Leeds. It was the brief period when Gresley Class A3 Pacifics took over workings that since 1943 had been the preserve of rebuilt 'Scots'. The A3s had been displaced from the East Coast mainline by Deltics and English Electric type 4s, later class 40s.

Opposite, above

Steam was about to end and the Thames-Clyde Express was no longer non-stop from Leeds to Carlisle when Type 4 diesel No. D21 called at Skipton station on 18th March 1967 with the northbound train.

Economies were now in full force, with passenger services from Skipton to Ilkley ceasing in 1965 to be followed five years later by those to Colne. The track layout is as yet little changed. Soaring skywards at top left is the 225-feet-high chimney of Dewhurst's cotton mill.

Below

Sadly, the Thames-Clyde Express failed by just one year to achieve a half-century since receiving its name in 1927. Through services between London St Pancras and Glasgow ended on 2nd May 1976 without ceremony. There was not even a special headboard on the last northbound train headed by class 45 No. 45071.

Here it is just west of Gargrave station where the infant River Aire in the foreground has left the scenic splendours of Malhamdale. In less than five miles it will be flowing past the outskirts of Skipton before meandering its way down Airedale to Keighley and Leeds.

Above

The end of the Thames-Clyde Express was scarcely mourned in the Aire Valley. Replacement Nottingham-Glasgow services initially seemed respectable until sacrificed in 1982 as a first stage of prolonged high drama and attempted closure of the Settle-Carlisle line.

In relatively calmer times the 10.20 from Nottingham is rounding the sharp curve at Shipley on 10th May 1978. Green fields and plenty of semaphore signals are still in evidence. Electrification and provision of platforms on this side of the Shipley triangle belong to the new age that was about to dawn.

Opposite, above

It took time for West Yorkshire PTE to make major changes following its formation in 1974, although it was relatively quick to enhance its corporate image by adopting a new green and cream livery for diesel units on local services. In this June 1979 view at Guiseley Junction, the one on the left is leaving Shipley bound for Leeds. The other is taking the Ilkley branch. The magnificent array of junction signals still retain links with the old order, as in a different way do the factory chimney and gasometer in the background.

Opposite, below

Steps by the PTE to make radical improvements gathered strength in the 1980s. It was clearly a great occasion thronged with crowds for the reopening of Saltaire station on 9th April 1984.

Much had still to be done, with invited guests and dignitaries having the doubtful pleasure of travelling in 141 006 – one of the new class 141s that soon came to have a dreadful reputation for their ride quality.

A NEW AGE

333 016
Way out

Opposite, above

A very different scene at Saltaire in June 2010 with the vast Salts Mill in the background. It is fortunate in what is now a World Heritage Site that the overhead wires are not immediately obvious. They are part of the transformation that in 1995 brought electrified services running at frequent regular intervals along Airedale between Leeds, Bradford and Skipton.

A further massive upgrade in 2001 saw services handled by strikingly modern class 333 multiple units, newly built in Spain and sent to Leeds through the Channel Tunnel. No. 333 016 is here forming the 13.02 from Skipton to Bradford Forster Square.

Opposite, below

Prior to the arrival of the class 333s, there was a brief period that certainly did not help in promoting the benefits of electrification. The only available multiple units were those of Class 308, built as long ago as 1957 and 'cascaded' from the London, Tilbury & Southend line.

One such unit looks to be crossing a great lake when heading from Cononley to Skipton on 4th November 2000. Flooding in Airedale at this point is not uncommon, although it was certainly a winter when rainfall was above average.

Above

Another new station is Apperley Bridge, opened in 2015 with staggered platforms either side of the overbridge. An exact half-century had elapsed since the closure of its predecessor, half a mile to the east. A PTE Class 333 is forming a westbound service on 1st June 2021.

LOWER RIBBLESDALE

SKIPTON - HELLIFIELD - CLAPHAM

When a railway through Airedale from Leeds to Skipton and on to Colne was completed in 1848, it was already clear that a far greater ambition lay ahead. There was an obvious need for a line linking what was then the West Riding of Yorkshire with Scotland. Out of many schemes conceived during the 'railway mania', there emerged the North Western Railway. It was formed in 1846 to build a mainline extending from Skipton to cross the Pennine watershed at its lowest near Hellifield before entering Ribblesdale. It then ran alongside the southern and western edges of the Dales for most of its length. Passing close to Settle, a branch to Lancaster would diverge at Clapham. Its mainline would continue through Ingleton to a junction at Low Gill, 4½ miles south of Tebay, with the Lancaster & Carlisle Railway. This company formed a key component of the West Coast mainline and from its opening in December 1846 was worked by the London & North Western Railway – soon commonly known as the 'Premier Line'.

In contrast its potential neighbour gained the less impressive nickname of the 'little' North Western to avoid confusion between the two concerns. It proved small in terms of capital resources and difficult years following the 'railway mania' forced a total change in strategy. The Clapham to Low Gill section involved heavy engineering and it was decided it should be deferred in favour of completing a link with Lancaster. A connection could be made here with the West Coast mainline, and although it would now provide a less direct route to the north it would be much cheaper to build.

Services over the 25 miles from Skipton to Ingleton began in 1849 and a year later saw completion of what had become the main line from a junction at Clapham to Lancaster. There were now rail links to London and Scotland for both Skipton and Settle, two important gateway towns to the Dales. As the Midland Railway had already absorbed the line connecting Leeds and Skipton, it now arranged to work all traffic on the 'little' North Western, even though the indirect route northwards involved a change of trains at Lancaster and was far from ideal.

There matters stood until both the 'Premier Line' and the Midland promoted rival schemes for the missing link from Ingleton to Low Gill. Parliament preferred the former and Yorkshire folk no doubt looked forward to much easier journeys to Scotland.

Unfortunately they were to be frustrated by the divisive railway politics of the mid-nineteenth century. Ingleton was now destined to be a railway frontier between two major and increasingly hostile companies. There was little incentive to complete the 22-mile Ingleton to Low Gill link but it was finally opened as an unimportant branch line in September 1861. Although they may be slightly exaggerated, many pen pictures have been painted of passengers having to leave their Midland train at Ingleton and get to the separate 'Premier Line' station only to see the so-called 'connection' disappearing into the distance.

In a country with a government-controlled approach to railway development, there would have been a trunk mainline from Leeds to Carlisle via Ingleton and Low Gill. Put simply, it was the best, most direct and relatively low-lying route from the West Riding to Scotland. Yet two of the largest and most powerful railway companies in Britain refused to see it that way. Their constant rivalry and sheer obstinacy was to cast reasoning to one side and bring railways to the Dales from the periphery to the heartland. It led to the magnificent but unnecessary line from Settle to Carlisle passing through three Yorkshire dales, as described in later pages.

When the Midland completed its new route to Scotland in 1876, it changed the small village of Hellifield into a much larger railway settlement. The Lancashire & Yorkshire Railway, also at odds with the 'Premier Line', wanted to use the Settle-Carlisle for its traffic from Manchester to Scotland. Hellifield proved to be the most convenient point for a junction with associated engine sheds and also a new station, opened in 1880.

Once the Midland had its new Anglo-Scottish mainline, the older route westwards from Settle through Clapham developed mainly to serve Morecambe – first as a port and then a fashionable resort. Cheap holiday flights eventually brought a steady decline and it is now a line that survives with difficulty. In its Edwardian heyday through expresses from Bradford to Morecambe completed the journey in 90 minutes, but today it is likely to take three hours and involve two changes of train.

The Clapham to Low Gill line through Ingleton lost its local services in 1954 and was then retained for diversionary purposes. It proved valuable in the winters of 1947 and 1963 when the Settle-Carlisle was blocked by snow but such occasional traffic came to be seen as a luxury and it was completely closed in July 1966.

Plaques at Hellifield station commemorating its restoration in 1994.

Opposite, above

Hellifield station on 2nd May 1976. Although the bay platform to the right of the signal box is no longer in use, the layout has not greatly changed since opening in 1880. Diverging to the left is the now little used ex-Lancashire & Yorkshire line to Clitheroe and Blackburn.

The last up Thames-Clyde Express headed by class 45 No. 45073 is on its way to Leeds and London St Pancras.

Opposite, below

Not all passengers may have fancied a trip to Carlisle on a 'Pacer', but here a class 142 is heading a 156 as they approach Hellifield. They are forming the 10.49 from Leeds on 17th December 2005.

Above

Hellifield station, a broad island platform with a central two-storey building, boasts some pure Midland architecture. This includes a sloping glass canopy on decorative iron columns and brackets bearing the company's initials and Wyvern symbol.

After years of neglect, it was listed Grade II and excellently restored, as seen on completion of the work in 1994. Plans for other uses including offices were never fully realised but the station still has a café that receives high praise.

2N71

2N71

Opposite, above

The junction at the west end of Clapham station showed former hopes only too clearly. Running straight ahead towards Ingleton is what the Midland intended to be part of its mainline to Scotland. Rounding the curve is what was conceived as a branch but came to serve Morecambe.

Once the Settle-Carlisle line was opened, the route via Ingleton was retained for local services and diversions until closure in July 1966. Four months earlier, class 25 No. D7592 is heading a Morecambe to Leeds service on 12th March.

Opposite, below

The same train at Clapham station. Its seven corridor carriages were typical of the time and utterly civilised compared with what was to come.

Above

Three decades later there was just a two-car 'Pacer' on a Leeds to Morecambe service approaching Clapham in April 1992. Its commonly rough ride would be made even worse by the state of much of the track between Settle Junction and Carnforth.

Above

The unmistakable shape of Ingleborough provides a dramatic backdrop at Kettlebeck, between Settle and Clapham. An extremely rare working is this diverted Mossend to Margam steel train behind class 20s Nos. 20075 and 20073 on 11th March 1975. Only running for a few weekends, it was at over a thousand tonnes reputedly the heaviest train ever to work over the line.

Opposite, above

A far more common sight at Kettlebeck has been the Cumbrian Mountain Express. Class 5 No. 45407 is heading its Skipton to Carnforth run on 3rd May 1989.

Opposite, below

A symbolic view at Settle Junction of one of the most striking developments in the entire history of railways serving the Dales. On the left looking towards Clapham is the 1849 line intended to be part of a trunk route to Scotland. Curving away from it and already beginning a long 15-mile climb to Ribblehead is its legendary substitute from Settle to Carlisle, finally completed 37 years later.

'Pacer' No. 142083 is forming a Morecambe to Leeds service on 14th January 2000.

L M S
Leeds

THE WESTERN DALES

SETTLE TO KIRKBY STEPHEN

Asked to name their favourite Yorkshire dale, the majority would not pick Upper Ribblesdale or Dentdale or Garsdale. Yet to railway devotees there can be no question of their supreme importance. Running through them like a golden thread is a magnificent mainline. It is the Settle to Carlisle railway.

Misconceived at birth and ignored for the greater part of its life, it then hovered on the verge of extinction. It could so easily have become a defunct monument to Victorian free enterprise verging on the foolhardy. Instead, this epic railway was saved against what seemed insuperable odds and is now a national treasure.

Millions of words have in recent years been written about the ultimate creation of the Midland Railway – a venture so costly that there was no ceremony when it finally opened on 1st May 1876. Determined to reach Scotland, the Midland saw the Dales as no more than a mountain wilderness that had to be penetrated at all costs. The Settle to Carlisle railway [hereafter the S&C] was akin to a Roman road heading straight as an arrow to a distant destination with scant regard for anything on its way. For this reason, many accounts understandably concentrate on the line as a whole rather than emphasising its dale-by-dale features that are so important to photographers.

After diverging from the earlier Clapham line, the S&C passes Settle and begins a near-unbroken 15-mile climb at 1 in 100 through Upper Ribblesdale. In quick succession are two contrasting skew viaducts across the River Ribble before limestone country becomes increasingly spectacular.

The first of the Three Peaks – all over 2,000ft – soon looms into sight in the shape of Pen-y-ghent, which forms an unmistakable backdrop to photos of trains on the final stage of the climb.

Next come Ingleborough and Whernside, totally dwarfing the line's jewel in the crown. A quarter of a mile long and majestically curved, the 24 arches of Ribblehead Viaduct reach over 100 feet above the boggy moorland. It spans a notorious wind gap where westerly gales funnelling up from Morecambe Bay can exceed 100mph and in steam days often brought heavy trains to a halt.

From the wilds of Ribblehead set amid its great amphitheatre of high mountains, the S&C curves northwards to reach the railway outpost of Blea Moor (its name an appropriate corruption of 'bleak'). A place almost chilling in its remoteness and until recent times having no road access, it has always been a key location in terms of handling trains. The line finally ends its long climb by entering deep and dank

Blea Moor Tunnel, almost 1½ miles in length.

The northern exit from the tunnel is one of the great dramatic moments of the S&C with the railway running on a shelf high above green and winding Dentdale. There are magnificent views, especially from Dent Head and Arten Gill Viaducts. Not in the same league as Ribblehead, they are nevertheless on a scale that anywhere else would receive the highest praise. Dent station, highest on an English mainline at 1,145ft, is a full four miles away from the village and approached by a corkscrew climb from the valley floor.

The second of two major tunnels on the line is Risehill, taking it onto another shelf above straight and not-so-green Garsdale. Beyond the station of the same name is the twelve-arch Dandry Mire Viaduct, only built after a quarter of a million tons of earth had been built in an unsuccessful attempt to form an embankment.

A final climb leads through the short Moorcock and Shotlock Hill Tunnels to Ais Gill, at 1,169ft the highest summit on an English mainline. It is one of the great watersheds of northern England. Two rivers rise within yards of one another on nearby Lunds Fell. The Eden flows north to Carlisle and the Irish Sea; the Ure trails east ultimately to reach the Humber estuary and the North Sea.

From Ais Gill the S&C begins its long descent down Mallerstang to Kirkby Stephen. Again running on a shelf, this time on the flanks of 2,324ft Wild Boar Fell, it is a stretch of line that has never fully received its due. It may be because it is not in Yorkshire – a problem finally corrected in 2016 when, somewhere between a fudge and a compromise, the area officially became the Westmorland Dales forming part of the Yorkshire Dales National Park.

There can be no similar uncertainty about the standing of the S&C – it remains a magnificent railway and England's finest mainline.

Photographs on the following pages, covering the period from the end of the 1950s until recent times, fall into five sections:

'REAL' STEAM (pages 30 to 37)

The S&C was not regarded as a photographer's paradise for much of the period through to the 'end of steam' in August 1968. It did not stand comparison with the West Coast mainline over Shap where steam was in evidence until the last days and there was a far greater frequency of traffic. By comparison, hours could be spent on the bleak heights north of Settle without seeing a single train. There were occasional freights, just three expresses each way (one of them normally after dark) and a tiny handful of stopping services.

'Scot' and 'Jubilee' 4-6-0s handled most expresses until 1960, when steam passenger working on the S&C reached its greatest variety as it stood on the brink of dissolution. In 1961 some Gresley A3 Pacifics, displaced by 'Deltic' diesels on the East Coast mainline, began to work over Ais Gill from Holbeck shed. They were well received and, with Standard class 'Britannias' and 'Clans' also in regular use, the line provided a marvellous stomping ground for students of locomotive performance.

A delightful and leisurely way of sampling S&C splendours was to travel on a stopping train. One left Hellifield at around 12.0 noon but the full experience could only be gained by the late afternoon 'slow' from Bradford to Carlisle. A mixed train of passenger coaches and goods vans, it called at all 26 intermediate stations and took almost four hours.

The mainstay of freight working until the latter days of steam operation were 'Black Five' 4-6-0s and 8F 2-8-0s. Standard class 9F 2-10-0s provided a fitting epilogue and came to be long remembered as they roused the echoes in Mallerstang or trundled quietly over Arten Gill in the shadows of a Dentdale evening.

HARSH WINTERS (pages 38 to 43)

Long before Climate Change was recognised and then progressively elevated to Climate Crisis and Climate Catastrophe, there was a feeling on the heights of the S&C that severe winters were in decline. Snow fences were overwhelmed in 1947 when the line had to close for two months, but the years passed without another similar winter.

Then came January 1963, when an Edinburgh to London night train was stranded in a deep drift south of Risehill Tunnel and passengers had to await a heroic rescue. The line was blocked for almost a week, although at least the low-lying diversion route via Ingleton was still available.

Another bad winter came in 1979 when snow ploughs were kept busy and two separate 'rescue' operations were required. It may well be that such conditions will never return but there can be few absolute certainties. In early 2018 the 'Beast from the East' caused closure for several days and cut off small communities close to the line.

UPS AND DOWNS (pages 44 to 49)

Policy statements of the 1960s proposed that the S&C be closed and services diverted to the West Coast mainline. It proved to be the first of many occasions when a guardian angel took care of the line and it did not happen.

There appeared to be an upturn in 1966 when locomotive-hauled stopping trains were replaced by faster and more frequent DMUs. The scenic splendours of the S&C were not then fully appreciated or marketed and the ray of hope evaporated in 1970. Stopping services were withdrawn and all stations closed apart from Settle and Appleby. In terms of local traffic it proved difficult to argue with an official report stating that very severe hardship would be caused to very few people.

Ironically, electrification of the West Coast mainline brought a revival in S&C fortunes. Much traffic had to be diverted over Ais Gill while work was in progress and it became apparent that slow freight trains could not be interlaced with 100mph electric-hauled expresses. The S&C was upgraded and assumed a role it had not enjoyed for more than a decade. Symbolic of the time was the success of Dales Rail, which in 1975 saw the Yorkshire Dales National Park charter weekend trains between Leeds and Appleby. DMUs brought visitors to reopened stations on the higher reaches of the line and return workings enabled local residents deprived of public transport five years earlier to have a day out in the 'big city'.

Contrary to gloomy predictions of only a few years earlier, the S&C achieved its centenary on 1st May 1976. Two years later there was a far greater surprise when British Rail relaxed its ten-year steam ban. The railway that had become one of the great survivors was now entering a swansong with preserved locomotives at work in the most splendid of all settings. Especially successful and creating a cult following was the Cumbrian Mountain Express with its impressive variety of motive power enticing the faithful to gather by the lineside in massive numbers.

Yet freight traffic was gradually slipping away and by 1981 had dwindled to a fraction of former times. Then the bombshell broke. British Rail announced that Ribblehead Viaduct was rapidly coming to the end of its life – it would have to be replaced at enormous cost within five years or the line closed.

UNDER THREAT (pages 50 to 55)

There now began what were termed a series of 'dirty tricks' to justify closure. The three Nottingham to Glasgow expresses each way daily were diverted via the West Coast mainline and replaced by two Leeds to

Carlisle 'locals' running to times that seemed as slow and inconvenient as possible. The little remaining through freight traffic was also re-routed and S&C signalmen now sat for hours on end without a train in sight. Formal closure notices issued in August 1983 sparked the most determined opposition campaign of all time.

As a next step, British Rail appointed the legendary Ron Cotton as project manager to see through the S&C's demise. He proved to be a flawed choice and what was termed 'closure by stealth' backfired in no uncertain terms. A skilled marketing man, he increased trains to five each way, reopened intermediate stations on a daily basis and saw through a fivefold increase in passenger numbers. Steam-hauled specials also became evermore frequent on a line that remained under threat.

While these positive developments were taking place, British Rail and its opponents remained locked in conflict that seemed to drag on for eternity. Expert witnesses at closure hearings put forward convincing evidence that the costs of repairing Ribblehead Viaduct had been grossly overstated but there was still no clear future. The situation became increasingly political until April 1989 when those who had fought long and hard to save the line were taken by surprise. Michael Portillo announced to a delighted House of Commons that the Transport Secretary had refused consent to closure. There was widespread jubilation.

SAVED! (pages 56 to 64)

The S&C at long last moved forward on a new tide of optimism. British Rail restored Ribblehead Viaduct and reliable class 156 'Super Sprinters' gave far better views than the locomotive-hauled trains they replaced. The Friends of the Settle-Carlisle Line, which had played such a fundamental role in saving the railway, now teamed up with other bodies to transform its fortunes. It took on a more positive appearance in a myriad of ways.

Promotion on many fronts has increased the number of steam specials to an average of two per week in the summer months. Annual passenger numbers, which were a pathetic 35,000 back in 1970, had reached 450,000 in 1989 and are now well over a million.

Freight traffic has returned and there was great local satisfaction in 2016 when Arcow Quarry, near Horton-in-Ribblesdale, again began to send out stone by rail.

The S&C, once scarcely recognising the Dales as it took passengers to Scotland, now has a very different role. It instead provides a travel experience in its own right rather than solely a means of getting from A to B. Serving the Dales and one of Britain's finest National Parks, it has an assured future.

Above

By the mid-1960s former express locomotives had been relegated to more humble duties. On 12th March 1966, 'Britannia' No. 70052 *Firth of Tay* is taking the 12.0 noon 'all stations' from Hellifield to Carlisle across what has become the line's trademark – Ribblehead Viaduct.

Opposite, above

Once it was clear that steam was in its death throes, the last rites needed to be experienced whatever the location. The number of heads sticking out of the carriage windows also indicates that the spectacle was being cherished while it lasted. 'Jubilee' No. 45593 *Kolhapur* is passing the disused Ribblehead quarry sidings on 12th March 1967 in charge of a relief to the Thames-Clyde Express.

Below

Six years earlier in April 1961 the Thames-Clyde Express was the prestige train of the day, making its non-stop run from Leeds to Carlisle. Settle station is seen from the footplate of A3 No. 60082 *Neil Gow* as it powers north. It is the same locomotive that is shown in the Aire Valley pages taking this service out of Leeds.

Above

The other named train over the line was the Waverley, which as the name suggests ran north from Carlisle over the now closed route through the Borders to Edinburgh. The up service, headed by 'Jubilee' No. 45562 *Alberta*, is breasting the 1,169ft Ais Gill summit with apparent ease in May 1961. Drystone walls, as in the foreground, make the S&C blend in with the landscape far better than would wooden fencing. In the background is impressive Wild Boar Fell – a mountain finally given belated recognition in 2016 when it was embraced by the extended boundaries of the Yorkshire Dales National Park.

Below

The down Waverley crosses Arten Gill Viaduct behind 'Jubilee' No. 45566 *Queensland* from Leeds Holbeck in April 1961. Seen here from the road in the bottom of Dentdale, this is photographically a challenging location. As the rail approaches are not clearly visible from below, there is no prior indication that a train is coming and a constant state of high alert is required.

Above

A truly mixed freight with a variety of wagons that have now passed almost beyond recall. Class 5MT No. 45100 is approaching Horton-in-Ribblesdale station in May 1959 as it pounds up the 15-mile climb from Settle always known as the 'Long Drag' in steam days. On the right are goods sidings that included a connection to the limestone quarry. To the left is a classic Midland Railway signal box dating from 1896.

It adjoins the cattle dock, which once handled large quantities of livestock. There were just three pens, each holding only 60 sheep, and the real challenge came every December when a thousand or more were brought down from nearby hill farms for dispatch to winter quarters in the Eden Valley.

The stationmaster in 1959 was Jim Taylor, who was responsible for the stretch of line between Helwith Bridge and Selside. In human terms there were two clerks, two porters, eleven signalmen and twelve platelayers. Helped by his staff, he spent ten years making a station garden that won seventeen successive 'best-kept' competitions. When it was raining – as was so often the case – he staged photographic and abstract art exhibitions in the waiting room. Times were very different!

Below

Standard class 9F 2-10-0s became very much a staple feature of the S&C from the late 1950s, but less commonly seen were any of the ten locomotives originally – and unsuccessfully – fitted with Crosti boilers. No. 92021 looks to be in far from pristine condition as it laboriously climbs past Selside with a heavy freight from Stourton to Carlisle on 5th August 1967. It was withdrawn from service three months later. Partly obscured by smoke is Pen-y-ghent – at 2,273ft the lowest but certainly not the least shapely of the famous Three Peaks.

Opposite, above

For some twenty years from the mid-1950s until 1975 a major source of traffic on the S&C was anhydrite from the mine at Long Meg, north of Appleby. Worked by ICI, it was taken by regular train to Widnes for use in chemical processes. Class 8F No. 48358 is north of Horton-in-Ribblesdale as it returns with 'empties' on 3rd October 1959.

Above

'Britannia' No. 70029 *Shooting Star* is crossing the main A65 road through Settle with the 12.56pm freight from Stourton to Carlisle on 18th April 1967. Until the end of the year, this train was regularly worked by 'Britannias' prior to their withdrawal. No. 70029 was taken out of traffic in October 1967.

The viaduct, constructed in 1871, shows the attention to detail paid by the Midland Railway with use of both limestone and gritstone. The wider 37ft 8in skew span across the road adjoins five 30ft arches. There is also a four-arch Marshfield Viaduct in the centre of the town. They form part of the necessity to maintain a ruling 1 in 100 gradient over the entire 15 miles from Settle Junction to Blea Moor Tunnel. It involved tipping vast quantities of material in Settle that also created a spacious site for the station and its goods yard.

75019

48321

Opposite, above

The last day of steam-hauled freight over the S&C proved to be 31st May 1968. It came as a surprise when Standard class 4 No. 75019 was diagrammed to work the morning stone train from Swinden Quarry right through to Appleby. It is near Stainforth Sidings as it climbed the 'Long Drag' at a steady but slow pace. A co-operative crew entered into the spirit of the occasion and enabled evocative photographs to be taken.

Opposite, below

Heavy and slow-moving freight traffic was often routed over the S&C in the late 1960s to keep it clear of the busy West Coast main line. This in turn was requiring major renewals prior to electrification, with track here being taken north by a pair of class 8Fs Nos. 48321 and 48758. They are passing Helwith Bridge on 24th June 1967.

Above

Another sad day in the calendar was 30th September 1967, which marked the official end of steam in Yorkshire's West Riding. The 1.30pm freight from Hunslet to Carlisle nears Stainforth headed by specially cleaned 'Jubilee' No. 45562 *Alberta* (making another of several appearances in these pages).

HARSH WINTERS

Above

The snow fences at Dent, seen on the right of this photograph, were overwhelmed in 1947 when the line had to close for two months. As they had not served their purpose they were allowed to slip into decay but would have helped in the next serious winter of 1963 when the line was blocked for almost a week.

The S&C had just been reopened when 'Jubilee' No. 45737 *Atlas* passes through Dent station with an up freight on 26th January. Getting up the 1 in 5 corkscrew road to take this photograph proved a daunting challenge. It was only achieved by putting scrap metal in the car boot, which in the VW 'Beatle' was at the front!

Right

The famous Dent station signboard as it looked in 1988.

Above

The winter of 1969 also had its bleak spells. Class 40 No. D236 leaves Risehill Tunnel on 15th February with a soda ash train from Larbert, near Stirling. The tank wagons still had a long way to go, as their eventual destination was Wallerscote chemical works in East Anglia.

Below

Class 40 No. D208 emerges from the north portal of Blea Moor Tunnel with a down freight on the same date in February 1969. Standing out in the snow is the drystone wall circling the tunnel mouth at a safe distance on stable ground.

4472

4472

Opposite, above

The most famous engine of them all – No. 4472 *Flying Scotsman* carrying a Queen of Scots headboard – performs strange manoeuvres at Garsdale on 30th January 1983. The station was chosen for the annual meeting of the Steam Locomotive Operators' Association and its members had no doubts at all about the most appropriate way to arrive. The space on the right was formerly occupied by the Wensleydale branch, trailing down to Hawes until its closure in 1959.

Opposite, below

The exposed Garsdale station platforms look distinctly chilly on the occasion of the SLOA annual meeting in January 1983. *Flying Scotsman* is alongside the signal box, the roof of which is just visible on the left. The far side of the island platform on the right was primarily for use by Wensleydale branch services. It was all too familiar to passengers who in winter would often shiver waiting for a mainline connection.

Above

Class 5MT No. 4767 heading the up Cumbrian Mountain Express scatters lying snow in February 1981 as it passes Kirkby Stephen. The town is now recognised as the gateway to Mallerstang, which since 2016 has deservedly formed part of the Yorkshire Dales National Park. A lasting drawback is that the station is a good 1½ miles from the town centre – a legacy of determination by the Midland Railway to head straight towards Scotland rather than serve communities on the way.

Opposite, above

Snow at lower altitudes in Upper Ribblesdale can often be little more than a dusting when the Three Peaks by contrast look ever more impressive. Class 47 No. D1545, climbing towards Ribblehead, passes Pen-y-ghent in its full winter guise. It is highly probable that conditions on the summit would fully justify its ancient name – 'hill of the winds'.

Opposite, below

The great bulk of Whernside with a white cap of snow making it seem much higher than its actual 2,419ft. This photograph from April 1983 cannot be repeated, as it shows two trains crossing on Ribblehead Viaduct which now has only single track. Both are diverted West Coast mainline expresses headed by class 47/4s – Nos. 47444 on the left and 47518 on the right.

Above

Winter can commonly extend into spring in the higher reaches of the Dales and drenching rain can be just as dismal as snow. Such seemed unlikely to be the case in 1976, when superb spring weather preceded a gloriously hot summer. One day that proved a dreadful exception was 1st May – centenary of the S&C opening. It was perhaps appropriate for a line that had always battled against the elements, but meant conditions were grim when two lengthy special trains paused on the short platforms at Dent made a strange sight.

Above

The end of steam in 1968 made the S&C a very different place with class 40 diesels becoming the staple motive power on a gradually diminishing volume of freight traffic. No. 40175 is in charge of a lengthy train of mainly four-wheeled vans and wagons in June 1979. It is viewed from the B6479 up Ribblesdale close to Stainforth Sidings, which originally served the quarrying operations of Craven Lime Works and provided outgoing traffic via Settle from 1873 well before the rest of the line opened.

The quarry became famous for its enormous and still surviving Hoffman kiln, named after its German inventor Friedrich Hoffman. Over 150ft long by 50ft wide, it used an industrial-scale process and could burn continuously for six weeks. Working conditions were grim and men handling burnt lime had to protect their hands with strips of leather made from the uppers of clogs or shoes. They needed more than a mere pint of beer when they had finished their shift!

Opposite, above

The road enabled a slow-moving freight to be 'chased' and photographed more than once as it climbed up the steady 1 in 100 towards Ribblehead. The same train is seen eight miles further north at the hamlet of Selside.

This picturesque location belies a looming tragedy destined radically to change the appearance of much of the Dales. Ash dieback, a virulent fungal infection with no known cure, is sweeping its way through the land and the outlook seems bleak. The mature ash in this picture has already had to be severely trimmed and, as with most such trees, a lingering death is the likely future.

Below

By August 1981, British Rail had a firm intent to close the S&C and through freight was becoming a rare sight. A down goods is crossing the River Ribble at Helwith Bridge behind No. 40094. From this viewpoint, Pen-y-ghent seems closest to the long-held but perhaps fanciful allusion of resembling a crouching lion. At a more humdrum level the viaduct shows how the Midland used red brick as well as local stone.

Above

When British Rail ended its ten-year steam ban on the S&C in 1978 it unleashed a pent-up demand for charter trains and the line soon became a prime choice for such workings. It was not always straightforward. There was a truly pyrotechnic display on 1st November 1980 when 'Coronation' class No. 46229 *Duchess of Hamilton* stalled on autumn leaves near Taitlands Tunnel at Stainforth. It had to be banked up the 'Long Drag' by a class 40 diesel.

Opposite, above

Especially popular was the introduction in 1980 of the Cumbrian Mountain Express, steam-worked from Carlisle to Skipton and then back through Hellifield to Carnforth. A return to the 'Border City' by electric haulage over Shap completed a memorable round trip. Weather conditions were at their finest on 26th August 1981 when A4 No. 4498 *Sir Nigel Gresley* heads out of Risehill Tunnel towards Dent station. Heather still in bloom provides a striking contrast with its 'garter blue' LNER livery.

Opposite, below

A week later on 2nd September, class 5MT No. 5407 is in charge of a twelve-coach train as it crosses Arten Gill Viaduct. The weather is again settled and some passengers must have assumed that in the Dales it never rains!

Nº 4498

Above

A rare moment of glorious weather at Ribblehead Viaduct when the sun follows A4 *Sir Nigel Gresley* crossing the 24 arches on 28th November 1981. It gave temporary cheer to gloomy hearts, as the bombshell had just broken that alleged serious structural decay would require either its replacement within five years or closure of the line. In this sunshine and shadow it looks at its most majestic with cars parked close to one of the piers giving a sense of scale.

Below

As closure seemed ever more likely, there was a dramatic increase in the number of railtours in the final months of 1981. One of the most notable diesel workings saw No. 55009 *Alycidon* powering the Deltic Cumbrian on 24th November. It is passing Dent signal box, closed the previous January.

Above

In late 1981 the likely future of the S&C took another turn for the worse when it was announced that the three through expresses each way between Nottingham and Glasgow would be diverted to the West Coast mainline. Prospects looked bleak when class 47 No. 47157 takes a Glasgow service through Kirkby Stephen in September 1981. Just visible in the distance above the last carriage is the then relatively new signal box opened in 1974.

The station had been closed in 1970 when stopping trains were withdrawn to leave only Settle and Appleby still open on the S&C. It was once unique on the entire length of the line in having a 1st class waiting room. On the right is the start of a row of single-storey cottages for workers, which contrasted with a nearby two-storey terrace for railway families. As befitted his status, the stationmaster had a separate and much larger house.

Below

Class 40 No. 40057 is drifting down towards Settle Junction in August 1981 when freight traffic was getting sufficiently uncommon to attract attention. The Clapham line is on the left and the start of the unremitting 1 in 100 climb to Ribblehead is clearly evident. The great bulk of Pen-y-ghent is visible in the distance beyond the buildings of Lodge Farm.

Above

One of the last through Glasgow to Nottingham buffet-car expresses at the end of the winter timetable on 2nd May 1982. A few lays later there would be a substitute 'local' service limited to a couple of trains each way between Carlisle and Leeds.

Class 47 No. 47480 is starting to run up Mallerstang and has just left the 424yd Birkett Tunnel. Despite its short length, it posed many problems during construction as a result of encountering shale, mountain and magnesium limestone, slate, grit, iron, coal and lead ore.

Opposite, above

Class 31 No. 31207 brings the late afternoon 'local' service from Carlisle into Settle in May 1983. The station buildings are of the same more generous size as those at Kirkby Stephen and Appleby – the only other market towns in the entire 72 miles of the S&C. Distinctive features are the gable bargeboards, the jumble of chimneys and roofs with an unusually steep pitch to cope with extremes of northern weather.

Below

Although the last through freight traffic over the S&C ran in the first half of 1983, there were still occasional diversions to occupy signalmen otherwise left with handling only four trains a day. Class 40 No. 40074 has been re-routed from the West Coast mainline on 24th April 1983 and is approaching Dent with empty newspaper vans from Perth to the depot at Manchester Red Bank.

Above

Strange events in 1983 saw British Rail issue formal closure notices and at the same time promote the S&C in all possible ways. There was always the feeling that closure was merely being deferred and hence increasing support for steam specials amid fears they would soon come to an end.

A favourite performer continued to be 'Coronation' class No. 46229 *Duchess of Hamilton*, which on 9th June 1984 put on an especially good display for the benefit of photographers at Ribblehead. It was still the days when specials were permitted to stop at the station, offload passengers and then reverse back onto the viaduct before doing a run-past.

Opposite, above

Superb light captures *Duchess of Hamilton* crossing Dandry Mire Viaduct with steam to spare on 29th October 1983. The 14-coach train is dwarfed by the slopes of Great Knoutberry Hill, deriving its name from a dialect word for rare cloudberries that grew on the fell. Local shepherds insisted that they tasted of 'nowt'!

Opposite, below

K1 No. 62005 heads a special arranged by its owners, the North Eastern Locomotive Preservation Group. Steam-worked from Hellifield to Carlisle, it is just north of Horton-in-Ribblesdale on 19th March 1983.

2005
L N E R

850

Opposite, above

Ex Southern Railway 4-6-0 No. 850 *Lord Nelson* passes the remote railway outpost of Blea Moor on 25th February 1984. The signal box, opposite the last carriage, is widely considered to be the most remote in England. Signalmen who work there need to be comfortable with the sounds of sheep and moorland birds rather than human company. In the distance is the unmistakable 2,373ft profile of snow-streaked Ingleborough.

Opposite, below

The 'Community Rail' special of 28th April 1984 emerges from the north portal of Blea Moor Tunnel behind class 47 No. 47211. The conifer plantation on the hillside was one of several on the higher reaches of the S&C then subject to much criticism due to the loss of mountain wilderness. Ironically, the line gained additional traffic when Ribblehead station became the railhead for timber extracted from Cam Forest at the top of Langstrothdale.

Above

West Country No. 34092 *City of Wells* in full cry near Stainforth on 7th April 1986. It was the month when long-delayed public hearings into the proposed closure of the S&C finally took place. Despite unprecedented and superbly orchestrated opposition, there were still fears that the end really was nigh.

Above

A combination of robust marketing and threatened closure meant that passengers using the S&C soared from 150,000 in 1985 to almost 500,000 in just four years. Yet its future was still shrouded in uncertainty when a class 108 DMU crosses Mallerstang Common on 27th March 1989. Only three weeks later came the surprise announcement that the government had refused consent to closure and there was widespread celebration. British Rail's attempts to close the line had lasted eight years – a year longer than it took the Midland to build it!

Opposite, above

Gradual transformation of the S&C following its reprieve saw the introduction in 1990 of class 156 'Super Sprinters' offering better window views and thus ideal for the line. A four-car service in March 2005 calls at Dent, increasingly a base for walks linked with rail services. Its claim to fame as the highest mainline station in England, four miles distant from the village it was built to serve, has special appeal in its own right.

The station buildings, latterly used for holiday accommodation, were sold in 2020 to the Friends of the Settle-Carlisle Line, which played such a crucial role in the long campaign to save the railway.

Opposite, below

A later generation of DMUs at Settle in October 2018. The station now looks extremely well kept with white-painted bargeboards and traditional lighting especially attractive. A final touch is flowers and bushes, provided by a local community group and reflecting a determination to restore station gardens wherever possible.

156484

158791
TRAINS TO LEEDS
Tickets
Information
Way out
Gentlemen
Ladies
Disabled
HOT & COLD DRINKS
SHOP

Opposite, above

The S&C retains its popularity for steam specials – or what are increasingly called 'heritage trains'. Almost certainly the only visit by an ex Great Western Railway 'King' occurred in typically terrible weather on 4th April 1998. No. 6024 *King Edward I* is coming off Ribblehead Viaduct, the structure that played such a pivotal role in the closure proposals.

Opposite, centre

Diesel haulage can also be far from conventional. Class 33s Nos. 33056 and 33008 are heading a Pathfinder tour just north of Selside on 30th July 1995. The front locomotive is in a Departmental allocated livery known as 'Dutch'.

Opposite, below

'Princess Royal' class No. 46203 *Princess Margaret Rose* approaches Horton-in-Ribblesdale on 24th September 1984. This black-and-white photograph captures the spirit of former times, as does the surviving stone-built barn forming part of Cragg Hill Farm.

Above

No. 4771 *Green Arrow* runs alongside the Clapham line as it nears Settle Junction with the Cumbrian Mountain Express on 22nd February 1990. The V2 achieved fame in S&C annals when in March 1978 it became the first locomotive to make a triumphant return after a steam ban lasting almost ten years. Unlike this scene, the weather was again abysmal with a misty 'white out' of driving snow to the despair of those who had braved the bleaker heights in hope of seeing steam at its finest.

Above

The same location can produce strikingly different photographs, as instanced overlooking the higher of the two viaducts at Sheriff Brow, north of Settle. On the late afternoon of 5th May 2007, a class 156 and two single-car class 153 DMUs in contrasting liveries first headed south with the 16.14 from Carlisle to Leeds.

Opposite, above

Soon afterwards there appeared the impressive sight of the diverted 13.00 from Euston to Glasgow. The class 390 Pendolino with pantographs lowered is being towed by class 57 No. 57316, both in eye-catching Virgin livery. It is proceeding at a leisurely pace, very different to the record set the previous year when one of these high-speed tilting trains travelled the 400 miles from Glasgow to London in five minutes under four hours.

Opposite, below

One of the most attractive features of the S&C is how it continues to blend into the surrounding landscape. Were it not for the class 158 and 153 DMUs it would scarcely be visible in this May 2009 panorama from the main road through Settle. The River Ribble tumbles over a weir in the foreground and beyond is the chimney of Waterside Mill, now a visitor centre and specialist clothing retailer.

Above

A welcome development has been the return of through freight traffic, although it remains erratic in volume. In a vivid yellow and orange livery that could scarcely be missed, Colas Rail Freight class 70 No. 70811 is hauling a timber train from Carlisle to Chirk, near Wrexham, in October 2018. It is near Helwith Bridge and, as always in this part of Ribblesdale, Pen-y-ghent dominates the scene.

Opposite, above

Even better received locally has been the re-connection of Arcow Quarry to the S&C, as it has reduced heavy lorry traffic through the centre of Settle. The link to north-facing points between Helwith Bridge and Horton-in-Ribblesdale was completed in 2016 and the quarry was soon dispatching much of its output by rail with most weekdays seeing two trainloads daily. Wagons are being loaded in October 2018 as GBRF No. 66748 waits to depart.

Opposite, below

The north-facing connection into Arcow Quarry means that most outward-bound stone trains have first to head in the wrong direction for seven miles before the locomotive can run round at Blea Moor. GBRF No. 66775 has reached Ribblehead and is about to perform this task on 24th October 2018.

66748
GB Railfreight
66775

Above

What is the finest prospect of the S&C to end this coverage of the Western Dales and the magnificent mainline through the mountains from Settle to Kirkby Stephen? Many would name Ribblehead Viaduct, but another clear contender has to be Dent Head Viaduct. This memorable scene on 15th January 2000 shows the green floor of Dentdale curving away to the left. At top right the line is high above the valley before passing Dent station and plunging into Risehill Tunnel. Passengers on the diverted 07.38 from Glasgow to Birmingham will be enjoying memorable views of snow-covered fells. The locomotive is class 47 No. 47565.

LOWER WHARFEDALE

LINES TO ILKLEY

It was the Victorian fad for retreating to a spa and 'taking the waters' that brought railways to Lower Wharfedale. A spring on Ilkley Moor was claimed to be excellent for those suffering from 'long confinement in populous towns, effects arising from late hours and the abuse of liquors'. Its properties were sufficient to impress Charles Darwin, seeking a cure from a mysterious ailment coinciding with publication of his controversial *On the Origin of Species*. The word spread with hypochondriacs of all kinds descending in the mid-nineteenth century on Ben Rhydding Hydro, with its baths of every description 'adapted to drive away dull care'. All that was needed was a railway to bring the great and the good to a spa soon to be known as 'the Malvern of the North'.

Local interests approached both the Midland and North Eastern Railways in 1859. Sensing that great opportunities might be round the corner, these normally warring companies for once agreed to sink their differences and adopted what the acerbic writer E L Ahrons described as 'a hostile courtesy'. It was agreed that the North Eastern would complete the first 3½ miles from a triangular junction with its Leeds-Harrogate line at Arthington as far as the ancient market town of Otley. The next six miles on to Ilkley would be constructed jointly. For its part the Midland would build a steeply graded six-mile connection from its Airedale line near Apperley through Guiseley to another triangular junction near Burley.

Passenger services to Otley began in February 1865 and Ilkley saw its first trains in August of the same year. Ben Rhydding Hydro soon had its own private station, complete with 'retiring room for ladies', where its clients were met by horse bus. Bradford had been promised the same rail facilities as Leeds for ease of reaching Ilkley and was only satisfied when a cut-off was opened from Shipley to Guiseley in December 1876.

Visitors now came in ever increasing numbers to the spa town. Many travelled in a reserved saloon carriage to Ilkley and then by wagonettes to Bolton Abbey, already made famous by Wordsworth, Turner and Ruskin. Pressure to make this scenic jewel more accessible led to the Midland providing it with a station on an 11½-mile link from Ilkley to Skipton completed in October 1888.

As with the Aire Valley mainline, the heyday of services came in the Edwardian era and included a summer Saturday St Pancras to Edinburgh express complete with restaurant car in those civilised days before pre-packed food. Calling at Ilkley, it reached Carlisle in a little over two hours – a journey time that is no longer remotely possible. During the reign of King George V there was always high alert at Bolton Abbey when a double-headed royal train brought him to stay with the Duke of Devonshire at Bolton Hall.

Gradual decline resulted in the 1963 Beeching Report recommending closure of all railways serving Lower Wharfedale. Ilkley mounted such strong protest that the Minister of Transport decided to defer withdrawal of services from Leeds and Bradford via Guiseley. The other lines were not so fortunate with passenger traffic ceasing in March 1965 from Leeds via Otley and also onwards from Ilkley to Skipton. On this section there has been gradual restoration by the Embsay & Bolton Abbey Steam Railway, completed in 1988, but unfortunately the goal of through services into Skipton has proved elusive.

Not until 1972 was the closure threat hanging over the services via Guiseley finally lifted. In the same way as the Aire Valley, a major step was the formation of the West Yorkshire PTE two years later. Improvements were made to intermediate stations and an hourly interval service introduced from Ilkley to both Leeds and Bradford. Passenger numbers doubled through the 1980s – and then came the real surprise.

Electrification of the Airedale mainline was certainly a welcome development but it was scarcely expected that Government approval would also embrace the Ilkley branch. Few railways have gone from likely closure to the benefits of electric traction in so short a time span. With preparatory work starting in the summer of 1992, the new timetable introduced in September 1995 increased trains to Leeds and Bradford every half hour. Operating at low fares, they provide Ilkley with a striking contrast to the once larger town of Otley, which chose to sacrifice its railway in favour of a bypass. Its inhabitants are now faced with nightmare rush-hour journeys followed by expensive parking fees.

LAST RITES

Opposite, above

When all lines to Ilkley were earmarked for closure under the infamous Beeching Report, it led to a farewell railtour that proved to be memorable in more ways than one! The RCTS 'Dalesman' tour of 4th May 1963, providing a first outing for preserved LNER K4 No. 3442 *The Great Marquess*, was certainly ambitious.

From Bradford Forster Square it headed through Shipley and Guiseley to Menston. It then made a detour to Arthington to cover the Leeds to Ilkley via Otley line, which had already seen its weekday services reduced to just three trains each way. All seemed to be going well when it headed through Otley with steam to spare.

Opposite, below

The Great Marquess turned on the triangle at Arthington so that the tour could resume the journey towards Ilkley. It first passed through Pool-in-Wharfedale, still a typical country station with 'period' lighting on the island platform and passengers using wooden boards to cross the tracks.

There is a distinctly 'time-to-spare' atmosphere, with goods being handled between a small lorry and a wagon parked in the siding. On the left are coal drops, which were a characteristic North Eastern Railway feature to ease deliveries.

In its heyday the station had facilities for handling high-grade stone lowered down from the top of nearby Otley Chevin on a rope-worked incline. These were long gone and few people had turned out to see the special. Today there is scarcely a trace that the station ever existed.

L N E R

RCTS
3442

Above

After running through Otley for a second time, the 'Dalesman' tour reached Ilkley and continued towards Skipton on another stretch of line that had already seen a reduction in services. At Embsay Junction there were further manoeuvres to go up the Grassington branch, diverging to the left in this picture and featured in the next section of this book.

Returning down the branch to arrive in Skipton, it was scarcely the end of the beginning. It was on to Earby to cover the similarly threatened Barnoldswick branch, down to Blackburn, northward to Hellifield over the little-used line from Clitheroe and finally back to Bradford. It was a grand tour that unfortunately ended two-and-a-half hours late with much of the final stages in darkness.

The Great Marquess was very badly off beat and to make it worse the Midland driver had never previously handled a Gresley locomotive. It may have looked splendid in its original LNER apple-green livery, but this should have been an early lesson in the saga of preservation. There is far more than the paintwork when restoring a steam locomotive to good working order.

Below

It was not the immediate end of all traffic when 22nd March 1965 saw the withdrawal of passenger services between Leeds and Ilkley via Otley, as well as those from Ilkley on to Skipton. The large Hawbank Quarry at Embsay, scarcely to be missed in the background of this picture, continued to dispatch ballast via Skipton for another three years.

There were also long-standing workings with the scary name of 'ammonia trains' conveying this essential product from Heysham to the ICI on Teesside. The route via Otley, Harrogate and Ripon conveniently avoided Leeds and York. One such train of tanks is approaching Embsay station on 11th May 1965 headed by English Electric type 3 (later class 37) No. D6779 of Thornaby shed.

Commonly double-headed in steam days, these heavy trains posed a major problem for diesel traction on the steep Wharfedale gradients. They were far from easy to stop! Hence the additional brake tenders, seen here between the tanks and the locomotive. Although providing additional braking power, it was no doubt a relief when this traffic was diverted via Leeds with effect from 5th July 1965.

Above

Diversion of the tanker trains paved the way for tracklifting to take place between Ilkley and Hawbank Quarry as well as on the line through Otley from Arthington. It was an especially sad sight at Otley on 22nd February 1966 with 8F No. 48352 of Stourton shed on a demolition train alongside the island platform with its awnings crudely knocked to the ground.

One brief lighter note amid all the gloom occurred a few months later in May 1966. Demolition work had then reached Pool and very early one morning a dairy farmer awoke to find a long line of wagons obstructing the crossing used by his dairy herd. Exactly what he had to say to Leeds Train Control cannot be repeated in a respectable book of this kind, but it resulted in a rescue locomotive hastily being dispatched from Holbeck shed at the unearthly hour of 5.30am!

Below

Otley station was swept away in favour of a bypass, but this 1996 view from a near-identical location clearly shows there would have been sufficient space to provide both a new road and a 'basic' rail terminus. It would have given the town continued rail access to both Leeds and Bradford via Guiseley.

1Z
76

INTERCITY
43107

Opposite, above

When Ilkley was determined not to go the same way as Otley and successfully fought a nine-year battle to retain rail services via Guiseley, there was understandably little celebration until victory was finally achieved.

A surprising event in the long period of uncertainty saw Guiseley station graced by 'Peak' diesel No. 25 (later class 45) on 29th June 1969. A railtour from Newcastle to the Worth Valley Railway was brought as far as Leeds by *Flying Scotsman*, which then had to give way to more humdrum motive power owing to engineering works in Thackley tunnel. The 'Peak' took the special up the Ilkley line as far as Guiseley, where it is seen running round before heading down through Baildon to rejoin the Airedale mainline at Shipley.

Flying Scotsman was later able to run light engine through Thackley tunnel and took the tour back to Newcastle via Accrington, Preston and Carlisle. It was organised by the North Eastern Locomotive Preservation Group.

Opposite, below

Well after the reprieve of lines into Ilkley via Guiseley, a similar detour was taken by a much longer Hertfordshire Railtour on 21st January 1989. Starting from St Pancras, an ever-versatile HST is entering Ilkley before reversing and continuing to the Worth Valley. At this point the front power car was No. 43107.

Above

Ilkley signal box, opened in 1913, was of non-standard design owing to the cramped location and had to overhang the main running line. After 80 years its days were distinctly numbered in this scene from May 1993 as work that was to transform lines to Ilkley on a once unimaginable scale was already in hand. A downside was that 'Pacer' 144 011 was to last very much longer!

ELECTRIFICATION

Above

What had previously seemed impossible had happened by 1995 and overhead wires were in position. Diesel units were still in the majority when West Yorkshire PTE 144 020 called at Menston on 26th May with an afternoon service from Bradford to Ilkley. Class 308 electric units were already beginning to appear and four months later they would take over most but not all services on the introduction of a new timetable.

Opposite, above

Electrification of single-track lines is not common and Baildon station between Shipley and Guiseley stands out from the crowd. It has had a chequered life, closing in 1953 before reopening four years later for just three months, and then finally seeing a permanent resumption of services in 1973. Pleasantly sited in wooded surroundings, there appears to be one passenger waiting for the arrival of Ilkley-bound 333 002 on 30th June 2010.

Opposite, below

The restored Ilkley station continues to reflect the Victorian character of much of the town. Midland-style glass and iron awnings have been retained and the overall roofed portion has become a shopping mall and travel centre. The former through platforms on the Skipton line are now a car park. Standing at the platform on 1st June 2021 is new EMU 331 108.

Way out

1
M&S FOOD
2
M&S FOODHALL
331 108
CAF

EMBSAY & BOLTON ABBEY STEAM RAILWAY

Opposite, above

Like many preservation schemes, the reopening of a portion of the Skipton-Ilkley line between Embsay and Bolton Abbey proved a protracted affair. Almost 30 years had elapsed since it was first mooted when this busy scene at Embsay was photographed on 13th September 1997. A Barclay diesel is shunting and on its left is a J94 0-6-0ST in pristine British Railways black livery.

Much needed covered accommodation for rolling stock is being erected. It contrasts with the Midland Railway signal box on the extreme right.

Opposite, below

On the same day, the smartly kept Bolton Abbey station reflects a great preservation success – even though it is a replica. The original buildings were in such a state of dilapidation that the only option was to set fire to them. Providing a sense of scale is the peak of Beamsley Beacon on the right.

The locomotive on a works train is No. 22, an Andrew Barclay 0-4-0ST built in 1952 for the National Coal Board and first used at East Hetton Colliery in County Durham. Its short wheelbase and limited coal capacity mean that it is unsuitable for hauling passenger trains on a regular basis.

Above

One of the historically most important pieces of rolling stock on the Embsay & Bolton Abbey Steam Railway has nothing to do with steam. The 1903 electric autocar was the first railway vehicle to carry its own internal combustion engine and generator to drive the transmission.

Built by the North Eastern Railway it became a forgotten holiday home and was rescued from a farmer's field. Its wooden bodywork required extensive restoration and in 2018 it deservedly won a Heritage Railway Association award for exceptional preservation work. In June 2019 it is seen at Embsay when working services to Bolton Abbey.

UPPER WHARFEDALE

THE GRASSINGTON BRANCH

Less than ten miles in length, the Grassington branch was all that belatedly emerged from a scheme to build what would have been a magnificent mainline through the heart of the Dales. A creature of the 'Railway Mania' years of the mid-1840s, when hundreds of wildly optimistic schemes were proposed, this one seemed to have the right credentials. It would have formed a direct link between Manchester and Newcastle – two of the great cities of northern England.

Drawing a straight line between them on a map goes plum through Upper Wharfedale. Thus was boldly conceived a railway that would leave the Skipton to Colne line at Elslack before passing close to Gargrave and Grassington. It would then run up the dale to Buckden, tunnel into Bishopdale and cross Wensleydale to connect with an existing line near Richmond.

Thus scarcely 50 miles of new railway would be needed and everything seemed to favour the grand plan. Although construction would be expensive, there was masses of 'cheap' money. There was also no amenity movement to make anguished protests about a line cutting through glorious limestone scenery. It was just one more symbol of economic expansion in the new and glorious age of Victorian progress. Surveyors duly started to stake out the route. Then came the Railway Mania's sudden collapse and the venture was abandoned never to be revived.

Had it been built the journey from Manchester to Newcastle would have been some 18 miles shorter than today's route via Leeds and York. Owners of mills in Skipton and lead mines around Grassington would have been delighted but others may have had mixed feelings. It had been a near thing, and just how close a call may not be appreciated by those who now revel in the scenic delights of Upper Wharfedale. A mainline railway would have transformed such a narrow valley beyond recognition.

Many abortive attempts were made down the years to build the missing link. They at last seemed to be getting somewhere when completion of the Ilkley to Skipton line provided the springboard for a branch from a junction near Embsay as far as Grassington. It was still seen as the first stage of a through route towards Darlington and hence there were great local celebrations when the optimistically titled Yorkshire Dales Railway was formed in 1897.

Once again all did not go well and it got off to a shaky start by choosing a local baronet as its chairman. Sir Mathew Wilson, aged only 22, was known as 'Scatters', partly through scattering his affections among unmarried ladies but also due to his hopeless approach in handling money. The financial affairs of the railway were soon in chaos and it was only rescued by support from the Midland, which worked all traffic from the opening on 30th July 1902.

It was now very late in the day for new railways, but at least the Grassington branch transformed the fortunes of the village by bringing in crowds of visitors. It also made commuting possible to Bradford as well as Skipton and the population doubled within twenty years. A wave of new housing included a terrace not far from the station which quickly gained the colourful nickname of Boiled Egg Row. In theory, dutiful wives saw the train arrive and could time an egg to be ready just as the husband crossed the threshold!

The railway never got beyond Grassington and its terminus on the opposite side of the river proved vulnerable in the age of the motor bus. Railway companies were soon investing in bus operators and regular passenger services were withdrawn after only 28 years. It was not long before the LMS local timetable made the picture only too clear. Two pages were devoted to Grassington and showed a full 'omnibus' service at least once every hour from Skipton.

Excursions remained popular among those who had always enjoyed day trips to Grassington. They resumed after the war on the never-to-be-forgotten Easter Monday of 1949 when a thousand passengers somehow crowded onto a train from Leeds. The goods locomotive hauling it was so severely winded on the climb out of Skipton that it arrived over an hour late. Waiting to meet it was the senior operating superintendent, whose apologies went down badly when it emerged he had driven there by car!

Such traffic continued into the 1960s. A handbill of Easter Monday 1961 shows excursion trains arriving in Grassington mid-morning from Leeds and Bradford. The outdoor movement was in full swing and there was a recommendation to take a ten-mile walk through 'the choicest scenery in Wharfedale' to Bolton Abbey. From here several late afternoon and evening trains were provided back to both cities.

The branch was still carrying ample mineral traffic thanks to its proximity to high-grade limestone. Immediately after its opening giant kilns were erected at Swinden, 1½ miles short of the terminus. The *Railway Magazine,* a publication expected to show bias in their favour, commented that they looked 'strangely out of place between the fields and the moorlands'.

A second quarrying enterprise at Skirethornes, connected to Grassington station by a rope-worked 2ft 6in gauge tramway, opened in 1904. It ceased to use rail transport in 1966, which was the beginning of the end for the branch beyond Swinden. Closure took place in August 1969 and the opportunity to develop a car-free approach to a key tourist destination in the Yorkshire Dales National Park was lost.

By contrast, the following year saw a massive expansion programme at Swinden, which was coupled with a determination to reduce lorry traffic on local roads. Extra sidings and a complete upgrade of the line from Skipton saw regular block trains, often of 34 loaded hoppers, that have continued to the present day.

Above

By 1965 the Grassington branch had been closed to regular passenger traffic for 35 years and its terminus handled just one goods train daily. Traffic was minimal, as clearly evident on 6th October when just a solitary wagon is being unloaded in a siding.

Only a few years earlier a station master, two porter signalmen and two goods porters were employed in jobs described as 'delightful and undemanding'. Incoming freight included coal, hundredweight bags of fertiliser and even ice cream in insulated black boxes, but now it was all fast slipping away.

Below

At least there had been an improvement in the motive power. Ex Midland Railway 0-6-0s, which had been dominant since opening of the branch, had given way to Standard class 4 4-6-0s.

No 75042 has moved its now empty wagon to the station platform and will shortly head back to Skipton. There always seemed time to spare, especially at certain times of year when the daily goods could take an age to arrive. The delay was only explained when the driver produced a bag of mushrooms picked from fields bordering the line!

Right

Returning to Skipton, No. 75042 passes the kilns of Swinden Quarry. Huge in size and completely at odds with what had become a National Park, they were ousted by a vast expansion of quarrying in the early 1970s that was to see most of the Grassington branch survive to the present day.

Below

In 1968 the branch briefly ceased to be a backwater and became a honeypot for photographers. By accident rather than design it proved to be the last steam-worked branch line in Britain with the class 4s from Carnforth shed specially spruced up by volunteer cleaning gangs.

On 15 August it was less than a month before the official 'end of steam' on British Railways. No. 75019 is getting to grips with a loaded train as it tackles the climb away from Swinden Quarry.

Opposite

There were established rites at the gated level crossing at Rylstone, which did well to retain its splendid Midland lower-quadrant signals provided for the opening of the line. No. 75019 came to a stop and the gates were closed to halt road traffic.

Above

The appropriate signal was then lowered and the class 4 prepared to take its train to the far side of the crossing. Once the brake van at the rear was clear, the signal would be raised and the gates opened.

60095
095

Opposite, above

Expansion of Swinden Quarry brought lengthy block trains of hoppers conveying stone to such destinations as Leeds and Hull. Some was also shipped to Goole for use in construction of the Humber Bridge.

Weighty trains well in excess of 2000 tonnes needed ample motive power, which at one stage was provided by a pair of class 31 diesels. No. 31108 is coupled to 31243 on a loaded train in February 1990. They are close to Crookrise and the 1 in 75 descent into Skipton, which in the opposite direction could be a severe trial in steam days.

Opposite, below

The 3,100hp class 60 Co-Cos were able to haul the block trains single-handed. No. 60095 was new and still in pristine condition when photographed at the quarry in July 1992. The industrial plant is massive but causes significantly less pollution than the ancient kilns it replaced.

Above

The surviving part of the branch between Skipton and Swinden Quarry retains several attractive features, as instanced by this S-shaped curve at Clints Rock, near Rylstone. No. 60027 threads between the drystone walls and disturbs the lambs as it heads towards Skipton bound for Hull in May 1995. The length of the train visibly demonstrates the number of lorry movements that it is saving on narrow Dales roads.

CONTRASTS IN RAILTOURS

Above

The summer of 1968 brought a prolific number of railtours as the end of steam approached. It had already been a long day for the RCTS tour of 16th June, which was diesel-hauled from Leeds as far as Stansfield Hall, near Todmorden. The acclaimed 'Britannia' Pacific No. 70013 *Oliver Cromwell* then took it forward to Carnforth and on to Skipton. Here class 24 diesel No. D5113 is bringing it to Grassington station before running round and returning to Leeds.

One is bound to wonder if the driver is anxiously looking out of the cab to see if the track still existed beneath the weeds. Freight traffic beyond Swinden was now on its last days and was to end little more than a year later. The timber station buildings, erected in 1902 as an economy measure at a cost of £279, were rapidly deteriorating and were demolished in the mid-1970s.

Opposite, above

The sleek length of an HST looks strangely incongruous at Swinden Quarry on 26th January 1991. The Mills and Dales Tour had left St Pancras at 7.33am and ran via Sheffield, Penistone and Wakefield to Skipton before running up the branch. It was back in London at 22.05.

Opposite, below

A four-car diesel unit heads up the branch on 7th August 1997. Prominent in the distance is the distinctive outline of Embsay Crag. Such striking scenery has led to repeated calls for reinstatement of more regular passenger workings, if only to provide a way of bringing visitors into the National Park.

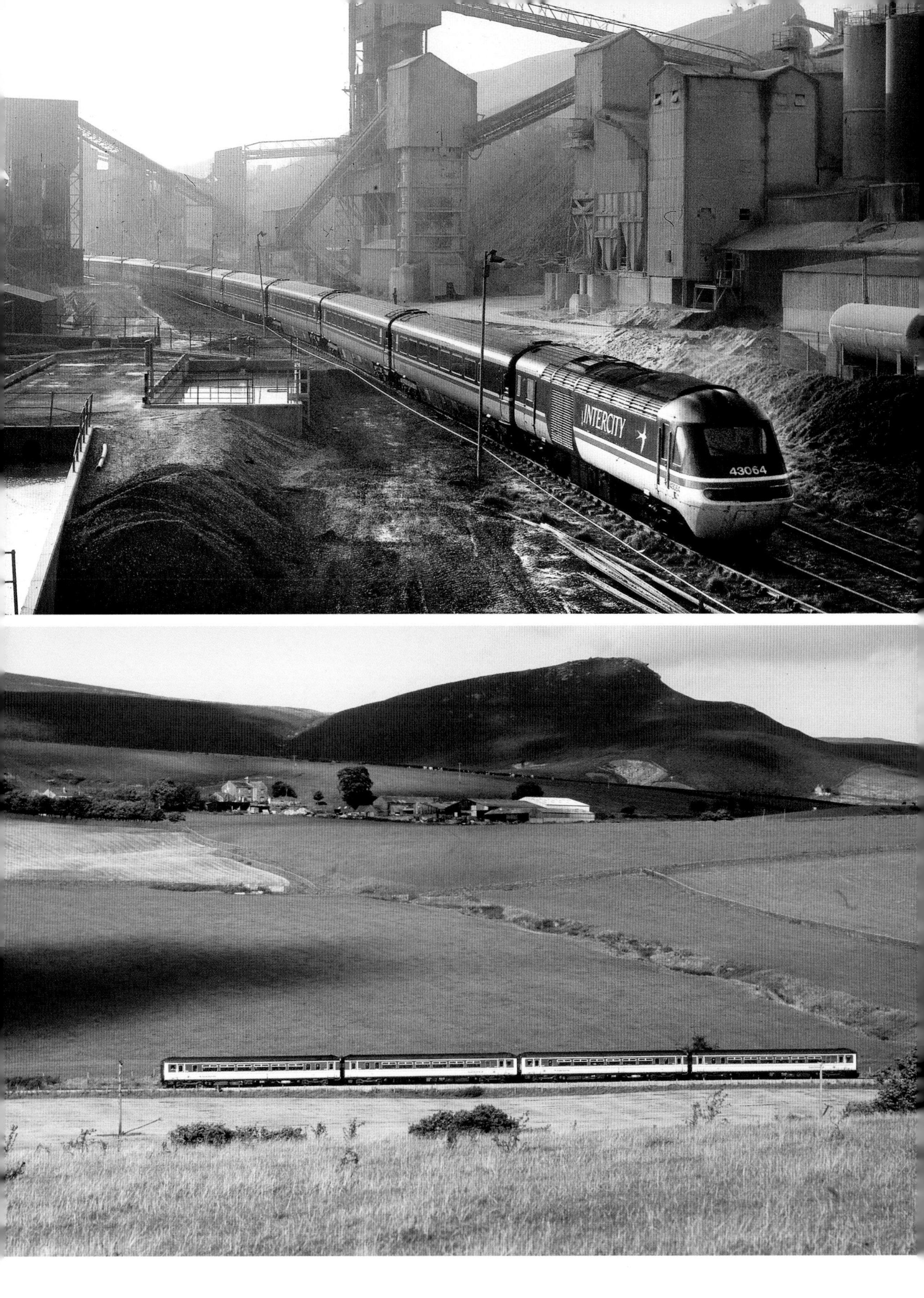
INTERCITY
43064

The DMU working up the branch on 7th August 1997 is approaching the site of Embsay Junction. Sadly, there is no longer a connection with the Embsay & Bolton Abbey Steam Railway, the track of which is just visible through the trees beyond the train.

EAST OF THE DALES

LEEDS TO HARROGATE

There were close similarities between railways on the western edge of the Dales and those on the eastern side. Both grew out of fierce inter-company rivalry and both met a desire to serve a spa town. The prime difference was that railway feuding on the east came much earlier and the town was far larger. In the early 1840s, when Ilkley was still little more than a village, there were some 4,000 inhabitants in Harrogate and visitors were coming in large numbers to sample water from its wells.

It was sufficient to impress George Hudson, the 'railway king', who controlled much of the mainline from London to the North stretching through Derby and York to Newcastle. In 1845 he decided to build a branch from a junction at Church Fenton via Wetherby to Harrogate. Two major challenges had to be faced.

Harrogate is situated on a breezy plateau west of Nidderdale with steep slopes far from ideal for railway construction. Moreover, its heart was a 200-acre open space known as the Stray. Then as now, its retention was of near-sacred importance and building a railway across it was out of the question.

Hudson's company, the York & North Midland Railway, solved the first problem in style by erecting the magnificent Crimple Viaduct – 31 arches and 110ft high – so that in July 1848 it could enter the town at a high level. Siting its Brunswick terminus just outside the Stray's extreme western edge and placing the approach line in a tunnel for almost 300 yards met the second challenge.

Hudson was famous for his adage 'Make all railways come to York', giving preference to his native city. This was not at all to the liking of the inhabitants of Leeds, who were not prepared to be isolated and decided to promote their own direct route to the North. As a first stage, the Leeds & Thirsk Railway was formed in the same year as Hudson's Harrogate line. The difficulties it faced were in an altogether higher league.

In less than 40 miles it had to cross all five major rivers emerging from the Dales – the Aire, Wharfe, Nidd, Ure and Swale. Viaduct construction was on an even more heroic scale and, most demanding of all, it had to pierce the high ridge separating Airedale from Wharfedale. At 2 miles 241 yards, Bramhope Tunnel is longer than the later and more infamous Blea Moor on the Settle-Carlisle line. It took four years to complete and involved pumping out a mind-boggling 1,600 million gallons of water.

The tunnel delayed completion of the Leeds & Thirsk Railway until 9th July 1849, when three trains carrying two thousand shareholders made the return journey. Having climbed out of Leeds for five miles, the line descended through the tunnel on a 1 in 97 gradient before sweeping across Wharfedale on the gracefully curved Arthington Viaduct. It then ran under

Crimple Viaduct and skirted the high ground of Harrogate before continuing north via a station that formed an apology for the two places it purported to serve.

Named 'Harrogate & Knaresborough', it managed to be two miles distant from the centres of both these towns. There was constant criticism that connecting horse-drawn omnibuses were 'poor and inefficient with uncivil conductors who often overcharged'. The only alternative when travelling from Harrogate to Leeds was a rail journey of almost double the distance from Brunswick station with a change of trains at Church Fenton.

Signs of improvement seemed possible following the downfall of George Hudson. Although undoubtedly corrupt, he rightly foretold that struggling small companies had no future. In 1854, a merger to form the massive North Eastern Railway included the two competing concerns that inadequately served Harrogate. Yet any hopes that the new era would immediately herald a connecting line through the town centre met one serious obstacle. It was the Stray.

Argument over the evils of a railway across the precious green space lasted for eight years before a commonsense solution came to pass. Brunswick terminus was closed and the site added to the Stray to compensate for land taken in building a line from the southern end of its approach tunnel into a central station. High embankments on either side hid trains from view.

Services from Leeds via Arthington now ran over Crimple Viaduct, joined by a steep and sharply curved spur with a permanent 20mph speed restriction. Beyond the new station a line was continued to a triangular junction north of the previously optimistic Harrogate & Knaresborough, now realistically renamed Starbeck.

It was a landmark moment when these new lines were opened on 1st August 1862. Harrogate was at last well served by rail and could expand as a spa before becoming a 'des-res' dormitory town for both Leeds and Bradford. After a heyday that saw through Pullman services to both London and Glasgow, it has recently developed as a conference centre. Local trains to Leeds are frequent, but sadly they depart from a station bereft of its elegance. The rebuild of the mid-1990s was a sell-out to commercial interests that paid little heed to the past.

Opposite, above

The mainline on the eastern edge of the Dales had an equivalent to the Thames-Clyde Express – and it was definitely more upmarket. Introduced in 1928, the Queen of Scots Pullman ran from King's Cross to Leeds Central, where it reversed before continuing to Harrogate, Newcastle and Glasgow Queen Street. It had a shorter life than the Thames-Clyde and ceased running in 1964 owing to poor patronage north of Harrogate.

In charge of the northbound service as it leaves Leeds on 2nd October 1962 is the then new and unnamed 'Deltic' No. D9016. It was later named *Gordon Highlander*. At extreme right are the cramped confines of Central station, with platforms of insufficient length to fully accommodate many expresses. Few tears were shed when it closed in May 1967 and all services centralised at a single Leeds station.

Opposite, below

Harrogate services from Leeds initially run under the wires used by electrified workings along the Airedale line. Direct Rail Services class 57 No. 57308 is passing Armley with a Tour de France special to Harrogate on 5th July 2014.

D9016

CROWN
HOUSE
DIRECT RAIL
SERVICES
57308

Below

An HST with 43313 at the front end formed another Tour de France special on 5th July 2014. It is curving off the Harrogate line at a point where the Airedale line catenary is clearly visible at bottom left.

Opposite, above

Road congestion and a vastly improved service with a half-hour frequency has increased passenger usage of intermediate stations. One of them is Horsforth, which has also benefited from falling within the area covered by West Yorkshire PTE. There is no shortage of customers as DMU No. 170455 calls with a service into Leeds in September 2019.

Opposite, below

Over twenty years earlier there was a more subdued scene at Pannal station in April 1996. West Yorkshire PTE No. 144017 was forming a mid-morning service from Leeds to Harrogate.

2
1
170455

RESTAURANT
Way out
Avoiding steps

Above

No sooner has the Harrogate line begun to climb out of Leeds than it crosses the 48 arches of Kirkstall Road Viaduct (also known as Armley Viaduct). Over a quarter of a mile long, many of its 50ft high arches are hemmed in by modern industrial buildings but there is a welcome gap where the River Aire is spanned. Even though very different to the river that rises in the limestone heart of the Dales only 30 miles distant, it still has a distinctive character.

A class 170/4 DMU is heading towards Harrogate in September 2019.

Below

Industrial development is most dominant on the city-centre side of the viaduct. It contrasts with a bi-mode class 800 'Azuma' powered from both overhead wires and diesel generators for non-electrified track. In September 2021 it is providing a shuttle service between Leeds and Harrogate for a major cycling event.

Opposite

River and viaduct give an atmospheric setting for the National Railway Museum's 'King Arthur' *No. 777 Sir Lamiel*. It is hauling the Scarborough Spa Express on 25th July 1985.

SOUTHERN
777

Opposite, above

Arthington Viaduct with its 21 arches may not be as long as Kirkstall Road, but at 60 feet is higher and certainly in a setting where its majestic lines can be fully appreciated. Such is its scale that the 'Pacer' crossing with a Leeds to Harrogate service in July 1993 is only just discernible. Helping to give a sense of proportion are the farmhouse with its historic mullion windows as well as the distant landmark of Almscliff Crag.

Opposite, below

The point where Arthington Viaduct spans the River Wharfe, showing to good affect the segmented arches in buff-coloured stone that probably came from nearby Pool Bank quarry. The class 144 is heading towards Leeds in September 2004.

Above

The viaducts are visibly striking but for problems in construction do not compare with an engineering feat that is hidden away from most eyes. Piercing the watershed between Airedale and Lower Wharfedale, the 2 miles 241 yards of Bramhope tunnel required the labours of over 2,000 men and 400 horses toiling in terrible conditions that led to 23 fatalities. Its highly ornamental north portal includes a tall tower with rooms thought to have been provided at the insistence of the landowner. It is generally in deep shade and harder to photograph than its southern end, which is difficult enough as it is preceded by a deep cutting. It is perhaps symbolic that the keystone bears the Roman god Mercury, patron of travellers.

Work in the tunnel on 8th August 1980 meant that wrong-line working was in force. Closure of the direct route to the north through Ripon has left a Harrogate to Catterick troop special headed by class 40 No. 40152 with a highly roundabout journey.

Above

With its variety of engineering features, challenging gradients and a good mix of scenery, the Leeds to Harrogate line is often a popular choice for railtours.

On 6th October 1981, the preserved Midland Compound No. 1000 is taking a circular route from York and has just left Harrogate station to return to its starting point via Leeds. It is heading across the Stray, where local interests insisted on high embankments to hide the line from view.

Opposite, above

The Midland Compound had made an earlier appearance on 25th August 1976, when it was piloted by preserved London & North Western 2-4-0 No. 790 *Hardwicke.* Such memorable sights were due to an enlightened policy by the engineering team at the National Railway Museum and there is virtually no chance of them ever being repeated.

The two immaculate locomotives are emerging from Wescoe Hill Tunnel, only 100 yards in length, before crossing Arthington Viaduct.

Opposite, below

Although it is certainly a healthy town, Harrogate is prone to spells of bitter winter weather. Heavy snow caused problems for the RCTS Solway Ranger on 21st March 1965, but there was not a flake to be seen when it reached Northallerton. This dramatic view was taken from the footplate of A1 No. 60131 *Osprey* as it ran into Harrogate across the Stray.

Above

Harrogate station, looking towards Leeds in July 1993, when it was in the throes of redevelopment that to say the least was controversial. Critics condemned the office blocks and held that they had transformed 'one of the most pleasant stations in the region into a dreary eyesore, quite unworthy of the town'. Claims by British Railways that it formed 'a more efficient working unit' were deemed inappropriate in a Victorian spa town about to reinvent itself as a conference centre.

Especially criticised was the removal of roof and buildings and replacement by a small shelter on the platform used by almost all trains departing for Leeds. The result can clearly be seen on the left of this photograph.

HARROGATE TO NORTHALLERTON

North of Harrogate the line on to Northallerton was always seen as inferior in character and engineering achievements. Any doubts on this score were settled by a fundamental change in 1969. It ceased to exist.

All started well with the opening of the line from Harrogate to Thirsk in September 1848, almost a year ahead of completion from Leeds as a result of delays caused by Bramhope Tunnel. The major work was Nidd Viaduct with its seven arches almost 100 feet high, after which the crossings of the Ure and Swale rivers were relatively modest. The most important station en route was Ripon, where failure to adopt a more convenient site was blamed on the influential Dean and Chapter of the Cathedral.

The Leeds & Thirsk Railway seemed content with its lot and soon had greater ambitions. It renamed itself the Leeds Northern and by 1852 had extended through to Stockton in order to gain access to Hartlepool and its flourishing docks. It did so by diving under the East Coast mainline at Northallerton, where it had its own low-level station. This was reached by a more direct route from Ripon, leading to the type of country junction in the middle of nowhere that was once commonplace.

When a direct line was built northwards from Melmerby to Northallerton it left the original route into Thirsk as a lesser-used branch. Junction status was enhanced when Melmerby came to serve a second branch, opened to Masham in June 1875. It carried mainly agricultural traffic, although in the early 1900s was kept busy feeding a two-foot gauge line built to supply new reservoirs in remote Colsterdale.

It was the Masham branch that made the first dent in activities at Melmerby.

Like Grassington it was on the wrong side of the river for the place it purported to serve and thus lost its passenger services as early as January 1931. Seldom photographed, it continued to handle local goods until 1963. The role of Melmerby as a junction then ended, as all workings to Thirsk had ceased four years earlier.

It was perhaps an oversight that left it as one of only two passenger stations between Harrogate and Northallerton. Of far greater importance was Ripon, although here too there was by 1963 a sense of impending doom. The Queen of Scots Pullman had ceased to call at its inconvenient station and the once popular service from Newcastle to Liverpool via Sunderland had declined to one express each way.

Four years later, all passenger traffic between Harrogate and Northallerton ended on 6th March 1967 leaving just residual goods workings for another couple of years. Ripon had the rare and unenviable distinction of becoming a cathedral city with no railway.

45562

NIDD BRIDGE

Opposite, above

A unique and surprising sight at Wormald Green station on 30th May 1967 with 'Jubilee' No. 45562 *Alberta* hauling the Royal Train over a line that had closed to passengers almost three months earlier. It had brought the Duke of Edinburgh to Nidd Bridge station on a private visit to nearby Nidd Hall and is here working forward to run-round at Ripon.

The decision to allocate the Holbeck Jubilee to the train and have it specially cleaned was taken by Tom Greaves, the District Motive Power Superintendent at Leeds. It seems the Duke found time to have a chat about the locomotive with the driver, who tactfully replied that it was one of the 'Sandringham' class!

Opposite, below

Formal duties over, *Alberta* takes the empty train tender-first through Nidd Bridge on its way back to York. Questions remain as to how much the authorities in London knew about this last use of steam on a Royal Train at so late a date on a line closed to passenger traffic.

Above top

A class 101 DMU leaves Ripon station in May 1965 and heads onto the viaduct across the River Ure. On the extreme left is the approach road to the station, which unfortunately was three-quarters of a mile from the city centre. It was a drawback that played a part in the withdrawal of passenger services in March 1967.

Above lower

A Liverpool to Newcastle express, powered by English Electric Type 4 (later class 40) No. D238, crosses the River Ure in April 1965. Many Type 4 diesels were allocated to Gateshead shed and regularly worked these services until superseded by the class 46.

Visible through the viaduct is the ancient bridge then carrying the main road out of Ripon to the North. Today it is replaced by a bypass that has obliterated much of the railway trackbed, although a bridge over the River Skell was retained with its deck widened to take the new road.

Above

One of the Gateshead Type 4s, No. D244, leaving Ripon with a morning Newcastle to Liverpool express in April 1965. After years of neglect following closure, the station buildings received high praise for careful conversion into dwellings.

Below

The once busy country junction at Melmerby with its staggered mainline platforms was a mere shadow of its former self when a class 101 DMU heading towards Northallerton called on 3rd April 1965. Complete closure would come in less than two years, as freight traffic north of Ripon had ended in April 1964.

To the left of the signal is the trackbed of the Masham branch, which saw its last goods train in November 1963 and was an early casualty of bus competition when passenger services ceased on New Year's Day 1931. The station buildings sit on a broad platform, as to the right they served the line to Thirsk that saw its last train in September 1959.

Above

The low-level lines at Northallerton, which enabled traffic from Leeds via Harrogate to travel direct to Stockton and Middlesbrough by diving under the East Coast mainline. WD No. 90461 is heading an up steel freight past the steam shed in March 1961. The passenger station, clearly showing its elevated position, is to the right of the locomotive.

Below

K1 No. 62044 and Standard class 2MT No. 78010 at the steam shed in March 1962. Apart from the Harrogate line, it also provided locomotives for the Wensleydale branch.

LOWER NIDDERDALE

KNARESBOROUGH

No other Yorkshire dale has such a dramatic ending as Nidderdale. It is not just the gorge at Knaresborough with the historic town clinging to its side but the castellated viaduct providing a final flourish of magnificent proportions. Understandably it has always divided opinion. The eminent architectural historian Nikolaus Pevsner, writing in 1959, lamented 'one of the most notable railway crimes in England'. Sixty years earlier the prolific Yorkshire author Harry Speight felt it was 'in admirable keeping with the style of the ancient castle and town'. Appropriately enough, it had turbulent origins.

A market town and medieval stronghold going back to the thirteenth century, Knaresborough had a pedigree that made Harrogate seem a mere upstart. It was inevitable that it should attract competing schemes in the 'railway mania' period of the mid-1840s. Out of them emerged a Leeds & Thirsk Railway branch from what later became Starbeck, crossing the Nidd on a high viaduct to make an end-on junction with a line having a more ponderous title than it merited. The function of the East & West Yorkshire Junction Railway was solely to link the 15 miles separating York from Knaresborough.

The foundation stone of the great viaduct over the Nidd was laid with true Victorian ceremony on 5th April 1847. Local shops were closed, flags were flying, cannons firing and a band marched through the streets. All went well for almost a year until cracks began to appear in the arches and within hours the viaduct collapsed. Although there were no fatalities, it was the beginning of three years of chaos and disappointment.

The line from York was completed to a temporary terminus at Haya Park Lane a mile east of Knaresborough, but was so shoddily built that a Board of Trade inspector twice refused to sanction its opening. It finally took place on 30th October 1848, after the company

Opposite, above

Knaresborough station looking east towards the tunnel under the town centre. It is an 1865 replacement of more modest original buildings constructed in a time of strife between two rival companies. Preparing to depart in April 1996 with a service to Leeds is 'Pacer' No. 144017.

Opposite, below

The cramped site of Knaresborough station is only too evident as a DMU departs in July 1993 and heads onto the viaduct. On its right is the curious five-sided signal box attached to the end of a row of houses. It controls the level crossing over the narrow street of Kirkgate, where the sudden appearance of trains between buildings has long been an accepted feature of town life.

This platform for
trains to York
144017

Leeds
144015
Way out

Vying with Ribblehead Viaduct as one of the most photographed views in the Dales, the castellated arches of Knaresborough could scarcely have a more different setting. A thousand feet lower in altitude, the weather is definitely less extreme as seen here on a calm July morning in 2004. Reflected in the still waters of the River Nidd is a train that is not all it might seem.

This was the period when a top-and-tail working from York to Leeds via Harrogate then made a return trip to Carlisle. The 'top' has already crossed the viaduct and forming the 'tail' is EWS No. 37408 *Rannoch Moor.*

had illegally run a free train to take passengers to the Royal Show in York. Matters continued to go downhill and the company soon had only one locomotive, noted for hauling mixed passenger and goods trains at an average speed of four miles an hour.

It was a great relief when the last stone of the four-arch and 78ft high viaduct with its castellated parapet was laid early in 1851. In readiness for the final stages of completion a line was opened from Haya Park Lane through a short tunnel under the town centre to a permanent Knaresborough station on the edge of the Nidd gorge.

Continuation by what was now the Leeds Northern across the viaduct to a junction with its mainline on 18th August 1851 should have marked the beginning of a new era, but instead the company lost interest in what had become the most expensive of branch lines and only a few trains were operated. A final blow occurred when the line east of Knaresborough was taken over by its long-standing rival, the York & North Midland Railway. There was briefly an uneasy frontier until both companies became part of the North Eastern Railway in 1854.

Over the years a respectable local service was developed, a portent of the future occurring in 1932 when a Sentinel steam railcar was working every 30 minutes between Harrogate and Knaresborough. Much later the town became the destination of a DMU service from Leeds introduced in May 1984 on a half-hour frequency with trains hourly thence to York. Although it had been recommended for closure in the Beeching Report, the line was reprieved and survived to become an attractive secondary route retaining a traditional atmosphere such as semaphore signals and hand-operated level crossing gates.

UPPER NIDDERDALE

THE PATELEY BRIDGE BRANCH

A Nidderdale mill-owner was the driving force behind the Pateley Bridge branch. George Metcalfe goaded the North Eastern Railway into building the 11½ miles of single track from a junction with the Harrogate to Northallerton mainline at Nidd Bridge. Once half the capital had been raised locally, construction was straightforward as there were no special engineering features and no gradients steeper than 1 in 110. Station buildings were designed by the North Eastern architect Thomas Prosser in a style noted for its chunky stepped gables and still to be seen at Goathland on the North Yorkshire Moors Railway.

Following the opening on 1st May 1862, there were four passenger trains daily from Pateley Bridge to Harrogate and two every Wednesday for market day in Knaresborough. As devout Methodists, the Metcalfe family would be delighted that there was no Sunday service. They would be less pleased about the tendency of many local residents to get so drunk in Harrogate on a Saturday night that they missed the last train home. Local lore relates how the branch engine was specially fitted with a 'blood-curdling and ear-piercing whistle' that was sounded in time for them to pour out of the pubs and avoid a long walk back up the dale.

George Metcalfe also spearheaded the development of Scot Gate Quarries high on the east edge of Nidderdale. Wagons loaded with top-quality stone were lowered down to sidings at Pateley Bridge on an impressive self-acting incline with a gradient as steep as 1 in 3. The output went to construct station platforms throughout Britain as well as such notable buildings as Victoria station and the National Gallery in London.

There might have been the familiar pattern of the rise and fall of a typical country branch had it not been for one unexpected development. Twenty miles south for a straight-flying crow was Bradford, which by the end of the nineteenth century was capital of the wool world. Massive expansion meant it was getting short of water and casting around for a site for suitable reservoirs. It settled on a desolate and windswept location where the River Nidd rises in the rain shadow of Great Whernside. Twelve miles distant from Pateley Bridge, it was clear that a rail link would be required.

The upshot was the Nidd Valley Light Railway, extending as far as Lofthouse from where a contractor's line continued to the first reservoir site at Angram. It was the high noon of Bradford's prosperity and little expense was spared. Stations including a separate terminus at Pateley Bridge were fully signalled and had substantial two-storey buildings.

Opening in September 1907 was a memorable occasion with the Lord Mayor and Corporation of Bradford travelling with numerous guests to Pateley Bridge. From here the inaugural train included a specially constructed saloon displaying the city's coat-of-arms. It took the assembled company up to Angram where a village complete with school and hospital had been created to bring civilisation to the mountain wilderness. A sumptuous five-course lunch received universal approval with the sole exception of Bradford Temperance Council, which sent a written protest to the Corporation about the amount spent on 'intoxicating drinks'. In today's money it totalled over £16,000!

Claims of extravagance could scarcely be directed at the first two locomotives, which were a pair of the Metropolitan Railway's acclaimed 4-4-0 side tanks made surplus by electrification. Fully lined in Indian red livery they must have looked glorious if impracticable with their large 5ft 10in driving wheels. An ex Great Western Railway steam railmotor acquired from a scrap merchant eventually proved sufficient for most passenger services.

Trains were timed to connect with North Eastern arrivals at Pateley Bridge, but there were no through workings between the two systems. The five-minute walk between the two terminals was not signposted and there was a widespread feeling that more could have been done to develop tourism and excursion traffic.

In contrast, there was a constant exchange of freight including provisions for the workforce and construction materials, especially after work started in 1921 on a second larger reservoir at Scar House. An unforgettable sight and sound must have been heavy cement trains, often with two locomotives at the front and two at the back as they pounded up the 1 in 40 gradient beyond Lofthouse.

Bus competition led to the withdrawal of Nidd Valley Light Railway passenger services in January 1930, but another six years elapsed before work at Scar House was complete. The entire line was then closed and lifted, leaving the thought that had the timescale been different it would have made a perfect preserved railway.

The Pateley Bridge branch now settled down to a relatively humdrum existence. An amazing achievement was that for 33 years it was worked by the same locomotive. G5 0-4-4T No. 67253 had its own single-track engine shed. It says much for branch-line economics that this one engine provided employment for two drivers, two firemen and a cleaner who worked alone at night to prepare it for the first morning train down the line.

The familiar pattern of more convenient buses and lorries took its toll and by 1950 there were just two passenger services each way with an additional working on Saturdays. The branch was forecast to close the following year and the fatal day came on 30th March when No. 67253 was given the dubious honour of hauling the last train. Pick-up goods traffic gradually dwindled and by the early 1960s there was commonly the extravagant sight of a large K1 2-6-0 trundling up the branch to collect just a couple of wagons. A railtour, a train chartered by local schools and a final brake-van trip in October 1964 brought the end of the railway age in Upper Nidderdale after just over 100 years.

Opposite, above

Twelve years after closure to passengers, the RCTS ran a railtour up the Nidd Valley branch on 19th October 1963. Weed-grown tracks provided a sad sight at Pateley Bridge for participants stretching their legs before the return journey. Fowler 2-6-4T No. 42409 has run-round and is waiting patiently.

Opposite, below

A final working up the branch on 30th October 1964 was this brake-van trip, departing from Starbeck before leaving the Harrogate to Northallerton mainline at Ripley Junction. J27 No. 65894, now preserved, was the last member of its class still in service.

42409
RCTS

65894
STARBECK SOUTH

Above

Local schools enterprisingly banded together to charter a train and give their pupils a memorable trip from Pateley Bridge to Harrogate on 12th March 1964. Such was the interest that it required two 4-car DMUs coupled together as seen here at Dacre. Unsurprisingly, it led to calls that the branch should be reopened for regular passenger services.

Opposite, above

Earlier, the DMU special prepared to depart from Pateley Bridge. On its right is the typical North Eastern Railway goods shed and in the background are the station buildings of 1862.

Opposite centre

A pause at Birstwith station, where the siding has the last vestiges of goods traffic. The local flour mill once received extensive supplies of grain by rail. On the right is the Station Hotel – formerly much used by passengers waiting for a train to arrive.

Opposite, below

Departing from Birstwith towards Hampsthwaite before joining the mainline to Harrogate. It may not have been such a peaceful rural scene inside the train!

HARROGATE
B2
B2
STATION HOTEL
B2

Above

A scene that superbly captures the dying days of a country branch line. Apart from the group on the platform, there is little sign of life at Ripley Valley where the small goods yard closed in November 1961. Autumn leaves are falling and it is clearly a damp day as No. 65894 pauses with the final brake-van trip. Crossing the bridge in the background was the main road from Harrogate to Ripon.

The station had an uncertain identity, opening in 1862 as Killinghall to serve the village almost a mile to the south. It then briefly became Ripley Castle – the nearby stately home – before adopting its final name. The 'Valley' suffix was probably to avoid confusion with Ripley station in Derbyshire.

WENSLEYDALE

NORTHALLERTON TO HAWES

Wensleydale, widest and greenest of the dales, extends due east from the wild Pennine watershed through the market towns of Hawes and Leyburn before merging into the Vale of Mowbray close to Bedale. Fertile agricultural land made it an obvious target for railway speculators, but in both its conception and demise a line through Wensleydale proved to be protracted in the extreme.

Peak years of the 'railway mania' saw work start on a Bedale branch from the East Coast main line at Northallerton, but the subsequent slump meant that only six miles were completed and initial services in 1848 terminated in a field at Leeming close to the nearest road. Local pressure finally bought an extension to Bedale in 1855 and on to Leyburn a year later. By now the Wensleydale branch had become part of the North Eastern Railway.

There matters might have rested had not the Midland Railway gone ahead with the Settle-Carlisle line, which touched on the head of Wensleydale in using one of the great watersheds of northern England to reach its summit at Ais Gill. A short six-mile branch from its Anglo-Scottish main line merely to serve Hawes might have seemed perverse. In fact it was now the high noon of railway politics and its purpose was to stop the North Eastern extending through and beyond Wensleydale. The two companies eventually patched up their differences and a North Eastern line from Leyburn to a joint station with the Midland at Hawes was opened in 1878. After thirty years a railway through Wensleydale was finally completed.

It was never more than a modest and largely single-track cross-country route destined to grow old gracefully. The rich pastures of the dale meant that dairy traffic vied with passengers in importance and by the 1920s there was an express milk train that left Hawes every evening at 7.0pm. It reached Finsbury Park before 3.0am in time for bottling to form the morning 'pinta' for London's inhabitants. The other staple traffic was limestone from various quarries and especially from Redmire, which ultimately played a key role in saving the Wensleydale line from complete closure.

Passengers gradually slipped away and through services from Northallerton to the junction with the Settle-Carlisle line at Garsdale were withdrawn in 1954. Almost as an oversight, one train a day from Garsdale down to Hawes lasted for another five years. Pick-up goods traffic went the same way and the end came for the line west of Redmire in 1964.

Further run-down saw the remainder of the branch reduced to a long siding, existing solely to serve the quarry at Redmire, but here the position seemed secure. Demand for limestone was buoyant and by the late 1980s there was a daily 2,000-tonne train through to British Steel at Redcar. However, the handling facilities at Redmire were outmoded and in 1992 the decision was made to obtain supplies from other sources.

It seemed that the Wensleydale branch had finally breathed its last and was about to be consigned to history, but there then appeared a fairy godmother in the unexpected shape of the Ministry of Defence. Attempts to preserve the line were foundering when British Rail set an asking price of £1 million and it was a fortunate coincidence that the MoD was looking at rail transport rather than road to move military vehicles to Catterick Camp. Redmire, only a few miles distant, would be an ideal railhead. Exercise Iron Temper saw a trial run in November 1993 with 19 personnel carriers being successfully moved from Taunton.

Agreement was reached that the MoD would restore the line and retain the right to use it with the first movement of tanks taking place in April 1996. This paved the way for the Wensleydale Railway to begin passenger operations between Leeming Bar and Leyburn with a ceremonial reopening on 4th July 2003. Services were extended to Redmire the following year and then eastwards to Scruton in 2013.

Restoration of passenger workings into Northallerton on a permanent basis has proved elusive. As with most preserved railways, the Covid pandemic caused serious wounding and all traffic ceased in March 2020. Services over the three miles between Scruton and Bedale, operated by 'heritage' diesel units, were resumed at the 2021 Spring Bank Holiday weekend.

TOWARDS CLOSURE

Opposite, above

Withdrawal of passenger services over the full length of the Wensleydale line from Northallerton to Hawes in April 1954 left just one solitary working at its western end. This was a train from Hellifield that followed the Settle-Carlisle railway as far as Garsdale and then diverged down the six solitary miles to Hawes. It was due to arrive at 3.27pm and then a little over an hour later set off back again at 4.25pm. Unsurprisingly, passenger numbers were never huge and there was little opposition when this token service ended on 16th March 1959 and the line west of Hawes was completely closed.

Six months earlier had seen a typical scene on a wet 6th September 1958. Fairburn 2-6-4 tank No. 42051 from Hellifield shed has run round its train and is preparing to depart. To the end, the service was nicknamed 'Bonnyface' as it began the return journey at a time when many railwaymen finished work for the day. There is also a tale that it sardonically took its name from a particularly ugly permanent way inspector, who when travelling by train always had the upper part of his body outside the compartment window as he checked up on the work of the men.

Opposite, below

By the time No. 42051 was ready to leave Hawes, there was not a soul in sight apart from three men next to the engine. The car park was utterly deserted, but at least there was a good view of the station. The style of architecture became known as 'Derby Gothic', taking its name from the town where the Midland Railway had its headquarters. It made no attempt to harmonise with the local vernacular.

Quite what planners would say today if confronted with proposals to inflict such a structure on the cherished landscape of the Dales is best left to the imagination. It is a touch ironic that it now forms an integral part of the Countryside Museum run by the Yorkshire Dales National Park – the planning authority!

Above

Although 6th September 1958 was a typical day for the local service from Hellifield, it also saw a brief period of exceptional activity. As part of a drive to promote tourism in the Yorkshire Dales, a four-car class 108 diesel unit was chartered by Leeds Publicity Club to give participants a four-hour stay in Hawes. Vying with Alston and Princetown on Dartmoor as England's highest market town, it must have seemed a suitable destination and certainly it locally evoked memories of busier times.

The special ran outward via Ripon and returned via Settle, thus traversing lines from Harrogate to Northallerton and Redmire to Garsdale that have now ceased to exist. It was almost certainly the only DMU ever to visit Hawes.

Opposite, above

Black-and-white photography can sometimes be far more atmospheric than colour, as shown by this superb picture taken at Leyburn on 25th April 1964. It depicts class B16/2 No. 61435 in pouring rain heading 'The North Yorkshireman', a special organised by the West Riding Branch of the Railway Correspondence & Travel Society [RCTS].

It was the last train to work through to Hawes, as west of Redmire the pick-up goods traffic had gradually slipped away and the line was completely closed two days later on 27th April. The B16/2 is thought to have been the last member of its class in active service and was specially prepared for the occasion by Neville Hill shed in Leeds.

Although the most important settlement on the Wensleydale line, Leyburn strangely has the plainest station of them all with barrack-like grey stone structures simple to the point of austerity. The main station building, on the right in this photograph, has often been criticised as resembling a farmhouse.

Below

On 25th April 1964 the special had to complete complex manoeuvres in order to run-round its train at Hawes. Returning to Leyburn tender-first, it was still miserable and more than slightly damp when No. 61435 passed class 37 No. D6779 heading a permanent-way train. This was probably preparing for demolition work between Redmire and Hawes to start the following week.

QUARRY TRAFFIC

Opposite, above

Class 37/5s Nos. 37517 and 37519 in their smart grey livery with large logo and red stripe make an impressive sight as they arrive at Redmire on 30th April 1990. Limestone traffic had grown to the extent that daily trains of 36 hopper wagons required multiple heading. This working will have left British Steel at Redcar about 9.0am and normally reached Redmire by midday.

Opposite, below

The stone traffic may have been lucrative for British Rail, but unfortunately there was no significant investment in loading facilities at Redmire. In an age of a 'full trainload' system they belonged to a bygone era.

Quite what was involved can be seen in this second photograph taken on 30th April 1990. Incoming workings had to be split into three portions, each of which was shunted into elevated sidings seen on the right. From here they were released by gravity as required and then fed with stone from the loading tower, after which they ran into reception sidings visible beyond the class 37. More shunting was required to assemble a return train, which was then attached to the brake van. Positioned at the buffer stops, it too was not part of a 'modern' railway.

There should have been little surprise when British Steel announced early in 1992 that it intended to transfer all stone traffic from Redmire to road haulage.

Above

The prospect of 750-plus lorry movements a week on narrow Wensleydale roads caused dismay and much protest with a petition of over 7,000 signatures being presented to Parliament. Ultimately British Steel decided to get supplies from elsewhere – notably Hardendale Quarry near Penrith. Involving a much longer rail journey, it was seen as symbolising a lack of joined-up thinking by two nationalised bodies.

The last limestone train, named 'The Redmire Requiem', ran on 18th December 1992. By now, class 60 Co-Cos of 3,100hp had proved capable of hauling the 2,000-tonne loaded trains single-handed and two days earlier No. 60030 'Cir Mhor' is passing Bedale station with the inward empties.

SAVED BY THE ARMY

Below

Once the last limestone train had run in December 1992, the Wensleydale line soon became overgrown. Arrears of maintenance were only too evident by mid-1995 when the Ministry of Defence announced plans to use the Redmire branch as part of a nationwide Army transport network. It agreed to spend £750,000 on upgrading the line, which was clearly essential as shown by this scene at Bedale on 20th December 1995.

The level crossing controls traffic on the main A684 road through Bedale. The station can be seen beyond it, and to the right is the brick-built North Eastern Railway signal box of 1875 originally provided with 31 levers. In 1983 it became the only signal box on the line and in more recent times has been splendidly restored by volunteers following reopening by the Wensleydale Railway.

Opposite, above

Under the new arrangements the first run of a military train on 10th April 1996 was named 'The Bonnyface', recalling the nickname given many years earlier to the token passenger service from Hawes to Hellifield. Planned as the key stage of moving 'Warrior' armoured vehicles – popularly known as tanks – from Catterick Camp to Salisbury Plain, it was intended to be a memorable occasion. This indeed proved to be the case, but not in the way that was hoped!

The margin for fitting a 'Warrior' tank onto a 'KFA' well-wagon proved extremely tight. One of the drivers got it wrong and the tank fell sideways off the wagon, overturned down the embankment into a field and fortunately finished the right way up. There were no serious injuries.

The Army took the incident in its stride and soon had the tank climbing back up the embankment and onto track level for reloading. There was a different reaction from Railfreight Distribution, which had assembled a press corps that inevitably made fun of the event. It would presumably be a happier outcome for the farmer, who would no doubt be well compensated for damage to his field and fencing.

Below

All went well for the next tank train out of Redmire on 14th February 1997, although it is only too evident how perilously thin is the margin when fitting a tank onto a well-wagon. Loading-gauge requirements are also pushed to the limit and there have been reports of station canopies being demolished on the Salisbury-bound journey.

This view looks east towards Redmire station and shows the two Rail Freight Distribution class 47s Nos. 47033 and 47213 that top-and-tailed the train.

Above

Conspicuous in the background as the February 1997 tank train leaves Redmire is Bolton Castle. It has connections with military manoeuvres of a very different kind when the forces of King Henry VIII ordered its destruction. Later repaired, it became famous as the home in 1568 of Mary, Queen of Scots.

When the Wensleydale line was built, Lord Bolton as landowner was able to insist on special facilities at Wensley station, midway between Leyburn and Redmire. He was provided with a private waiting room, toilet and separate entrance onto the platform for the sole use of his family. Trains were instructed to await the arrival of the Bolton entourage – a provision that caused many problems down the years.

Below

The February 1997 tank train at Castle Hill Sidings, Northallerton, before heading south along the East Coast Main Line.

When denied access to Northallerton station, it was close to this point that the Wensleydale Railway opened a temporary platform in 2014. Known as Northallerton West, it was integrated into scheduled services the following year but it has not proved possible to maintain workings east of Scruton station.

RAILTOURS

Above

Railtours continued to use the Wensleydale branch after its closure to passengers, although 'The Northern Dales Tour' of 9th September 1972 is thought to have been the only occasion a DMU reached its enforced terminus at Redmire. A head poked out of virtually every window was characteristic of such occasions long before air-conditioning.

The four quarry reception sidings are on the right and trailing off the picture to their left is the start of a line giving access to them. Alongside the train are catch-points – once considered essential in such locations in case of runaway wagons. Beyond the DMU is the broad green floor of the widest of the dales. In the distance is the flat top of Addlebrough, noted for its traces of Iron Age settlement.

Organised by the RCTS West Riding Branch, the railtour originated from Leeds and went on to other lines closed to passengers. Visiting Eastgate in Weardale and Consett, it returned via the Leamside line to Ferryhill. On arriving back in Leeds it had covered 367 miles.

Above

The HST (High Speed Train) has deservedly gained a reputation as arguably the most successful form of motive power created by British Railways. Able to run at 125mph, it can also go virtually anywhere. This includes freight-only branches, as seen on 18th February 1990 when the Wensleydale line saw its first visit by an HST.

The unit at the rear is No. 43013, one of the few fitted with buffers and now operated by Network Rail. Its sleek outline contrasts with the medieval battlements of Bolton Castle looking out across the valley.

Below

The demise of stone traffic led to a series of railtours. The final quarry train had left Redmire two weeks earlier and the elevated sidings were empty when the last of them ran on 2nd January 1993. Headed by class 37s Nos. 37714 and 37884, the length of the 'Wensleydale Lament' greatly exceeded that of the platform. It was to be another five years before reopening by the MoD enabled specials to be resumed. On 28th February 1998 the 'Wensleydale Phoenix' from King's Cross to Redmire carried 620 passengers.

Above

An early 'farewell tour' was the 'Wensleydale Ranger' of 20th September 1992. It left King's Cross at 08.05 and had covered 510 miles by the time it returned at 22.26. Organised by Hertfordshire Railtours, it was certainly a long day out!

Class 47/4 No. 47501 is passing one of the distinctive limestone rock faces between Leyburn and Redmire. Two of Thornaby's class 20s Nos. 20092 and 20169 were also used on the Wensleydale section of the tour.

Below

The same rock face is seen in very different conditions on 29th December 1992. A pair of class 37s are returning towards Leyburn with the 'Black Cat' tour, which started at Crewe and had the Pilkington set of carriages.

Even though the land is getting waterlogged in wintry conditions, the sheep have supplementary feeding and there is ample shelter compared with often harsher conditions at the head of the valley. Hawes can in some years have almost double the rainfall of Leyburn, even though the two towns are only 16 miles apart.

Above

An HST in attractive East Midlands livery crosses the river at Morton-on-Swale with the 'Wensleydale Rambler' from St Pancras on 20th April 2013. This is the rear unit No. 43050 but a feature of HSTs is that it could equally well have been the front as the train made a return journey.

The River Swale, with wild water in its upper reaches, follows a meandering course once it enters the plain and does not join the Ure until close to Boroughbridge. The four-span girder bridge is one of the few features of special interest east of Bedale.

Opposite, above

Leyburn station on 19th April 2005 with both buildings and track much improved from previous near-dereliction. Almost two years had elapsed since the first scheduled passenger service on the Wensleydale Railway had been flagged off by William Hague MP on 4th July 2003. Formal ceremonies a month earlier, when ownership was handed over by Network Rail, even included a fly-past of aircraft from RAF Leeming.

Class 110 DMU No. 51813 is approaching on an afternoon service.

Opposite, below

Leeming Bar station on the same date with the view from the platform showing a Ruston diesel shunter. On the other side of the level crossing, class 37 No 37003 is on crew training on the section to Castle Hill Sidings at Northallerton.

Today it seems scarcely credible that until the 1950s this crossing formed part of the main A1 artery from London to Scotland. Frustrated motorists on the Great North Road vented their fury at long delays as trains trundled past at their own pace. On the far side of the crossing the Vale of Mowbray Bacon Factory became famous for its pork pies.

REOPENING

FURTHER READING

This book complements the author's earlier work *Rails in the Dales*, which is not primarily pictorial. It was published by the Railway & Canal Historical Society in 2017, and as might be expected from such a body it has a text looking in more detail at earlier times. It includes the Nidd Valley Light Railway, closed in the 1930s. Also covered is the Richmond branch which, although serving Swaledale, carried traffic based in Darlington and thus more closely related to County Durham.

In a different way it also complements Gavin Morrison's *Steam Photographer: My Favourite Pictures from the BR Era* (2021). More than 400 of his outstanding steam photos from the period between 1959 and 1968 are included, and as might be expected from a native Yorkshireman it has a distinctly northern flavour.

For general background on the area there is the author's *A Passion for the Dales*, published by Great Northern in 2020. A chapter is devoted to 'The Railway Age'. Also helpful is *The Discovery of the Yorkshire Dales: Six centuries of travellers' reports and eyewitness accounts* by Chris Park (2020). A chapter on railways and excursionists who used them is especially informative.

Looking at the various dales roughly in the order they feature in these pages, there is first Martin Bairstow's *The Railways through Airedale and Wharfedale* (2004). Beyond Skipton, the line past Hellifield to Clapham and beyond is covered by Donald Binns in *The "Little" North Western Railway* (1982).

The S&C has a vast literature. Especially recommended is Paul Salveson's *The Settle-Carlisle Railway* (2019). It places welcome emphasis on social history and also the traumatic events of the 1980s that finally led to a reprieve. A specific aspect of the S&C is evocatively featured in another Great Northern title *Thunder in the Mountains: The men who built Ribblehead* (2018). The acknowledged classic work is *North of Leeds: The Leeds-Settle-Carlisle Line and its Branches* by Peter E Baughan (2nd edition, 1987).

The same author covers lines to Ilkley and the Grassington branch in great detail in *The Railways of Wharfedale* (1969). There is also *The Yorkshire Dales Railway: The Grassington Branch* by Donald Binns (1990).

On the east side of the Dales, there are works by K Hoole, who as a North Eastern Railway historian always put this company's achievements ahead of all others. They include *Railways of the Yorkshire Dales* (2nd edition, 1978), which is not a source for anything related to the Midland! The same title was revived for a pictorial survey by Michael Blakemore (Great Northern, 2005). There is also Martin Bairstow's *Railways around Harrogate* (2 volumes, 1986/88).

Finally, Wensleydale has its own dedicated historian in Christine Hallas, who has written *The Wensleydale Railway* (Great Northern, 2004). There is also the more extensive *The Wensleydale Branch: An Updated History* (new edition, 2017).

[Many of the titles in this recommended list are now out-of-print but often obtainable via websites such as Abe Books – www.abebooks.co.uk]